THE GLOBALIST AGENDA 2.0: WAR, FOOD AND ENERGY CRISIS.

THE PUTIN-BILL GATES DEAL.

INTRODUCTION

If the pandemic was used to increase social control, advance the world government with the health excuse and destroy the economy with confinements, now a new stage begins in which inflation will serve to implement a new monetary order, but it will be a new dual East-West order, with the eastern side headed by China and Russia, and the western side led by the United States and Europe. This new dual order will not be based on two economic models, since the two economic models of the East and the West are very similar, but rather we are going to experience the fight for world finances, the fight for currency hegemony, with a dollar that its future is being played out by the actions of the White House itself and by the United States Treasury, and the rise of a new monetary standard that in principle was going to be produced in a few years, but that already has an embryo or project, having as protagonist not the yuan, but the ruble and raw materials. The West has the dollar and wants to sink countries with raw materials like Russia.

In the first two books of this series we talked about the fact that the financial, technological and political elites want to impose a New World Order in order to impose a global corporate socialism, that is, a socialism led by some elites together with the large business corporations, where most of the people are poorer, more controlled by this minority elite, and where nation states lose authority becoming mere protectors, in favor of a globalist supranational state or authority.

If in the first two books it was explained about the first part of the globalist agenda 2030 that has been carried out in the year 2020-2021 with the Covid pandemic-plandemic , in order to get used to confinements, to obey, to lose freedoms and to use and share our private digital health data in exchange for supposed health security or any other type, that is, in order to implement digital identities aiming to implement digital currencies issued by Central Banks in the medium term, making money disappear cash; the second part of the 2030 globalist agenda has begun in 2022 with Russia's first attack on Ukraine on February 24, 2022, with the inflation in prices in general and especially that of fuels and food, which was already taking place since the year 2021, the incipient breaks in the supply chains and the famines that are predicted in the short term.

Nothing that happens in this globalist agenda is by chance as we will demonstrate in this book, since Russia's attack on Ukraine had already been predicted by articles in the English magazine owned by the Rothchild banking family, the Economist, specifically the articles of the October 26, 2017, issue on Vladimir Putin, with the cover title "A Tsar is born". This Russian attack on Ukraine had also been communicated, for example, by Henry Kissinger to Bill Gates before 2013, since Kissinger is one of his favorite mentors as well as Putin's.

In addition, the destruction of Russia as an enemy to beat had been published in the report of January 1, 2019, (before the Covid plandemic, or planned pandemic) of the American corporation or "think tank" Rand, entitled "Overextending and unbalancing Russia", which pointed out that it had to be brought to a situation that would hit its gas and oil exports through economic sanctions, while among the steps that had to be taken to achieve it, included the European Union reducing its import of Russian gas, replacing it with liquefied natural gas from the United States. This report also says that Russia's image abroad must be damaged not only through propaganda, but also by prohibiting its participation in sporting events, which is exactly what is happening in 2022 with

Russia.

And not only did the current situation of sanctions against Russia appear in the Rand Corporation report, but also in the NATO 2030 report, dated November 25, 2020, in which NATO says it has reached out to Russia to cooperate, and as Putin has rejected it, then NATO has decided to reinforce its forces, raising the need to provide the allies with more nuclear capabilities

On the other hand, the famines that are going to occur in the coming months of 2022 as a result of the food crisis had already been predicted by Henry Kissinger, and in this way Bill Gates has already sold his shares in other sectors and began to buy lands in the United States since 2013, saying that he was doing it because he had been told that a great food crisis would come. For its part, the Economist magazine also released a cover on May 19, 2022, with the title of "The coming food catastrophe" illustrated by three ears of wheat with skulls and articles talking about future famines.

Previously, in October 2015, the Food Chain Reaction drill was officially produced, organized in 2015 by the World Wild Fund (WWF) and John Podesta's Center for American Progress, to analyze the consequences of a great famine that would take place in the period 2020-2030, whose similarities to the current crisis are unsettling and show how globalist elites use these war and hunger games to further their agenda, similar to how the Bill & Melinda Gates Foundation, the World Economic Forum and the John Hopkins University organized the Event 201 in October 2019, just a month and a half before the Covid plandemic broke out, simulating just a corononavirus pandemic .

In this way, the economic sanctions against Russia suppose the beginning of a financial war that the globalist elites want to take advantage of to start the "Great Reset ", as the World Economic Forum calls it. While famines, rationing and energy crises will be used to decimate the population as part of the 2030 globalist agenda, while implanting a new dual monetary system, in which digital currencies and the fight for raw materials will be the protagonists

We will reveal in this book NATO's program to become strong and prepare for a confrontation with China and prevent its rise as the first power. A struggle at an economic, geopolitical, health and digital level in which conventional war has less importance than in other world wars, although as we are seeing in Ukraine, it continues to be the driving force. Destroying Russia, sacrificing Europe using the alleged climate change or global warming caused by humans as an excuse, and setting up a New World Order are the objectives that Western elites want to achieve by 2030.

We will finally see how Bill Gates positioned himself after the fall of the former Soviet Union to establish a Windows monopoly in the new Russia, which he achieved with the help of Putin, who helped authoritatively control Microsoft software piracy, in return that the Kremlin received the operating system from Gates with the excuse of increasing the security of its citizens, but with the real objective of spying on and controlling them.

While in parallel Bill Gates, taking advantage of the artificially created tragedy of the energy and food crisis, built step by step a gigantic food empire thanks to privileged information, among other suppliers, provided by Putin, and with crucial partners that link him both to the Russian and the Ukrainian oligarchy, and to the most intimate surroundings of the Ukrainian president Volodymyr Zelenskyy. Gates began buying land in the United States in 2013, positioning himself as the main landowner in this nation, following the advice of his adviser, the former United States Secretary of State, Henry Kissinger, who stated: "If you control the oil, you control the nations, if you control food, you control people", which received the Nobel Peace Prize in 1973.

In addition Bill Gates with the coalition, Agra, formed by the Bill and Melinda Gates Foundation and the Rockefeller Foundation, for the Green Revolution in Africa, replaced in several African countries the local natural crops for crops with transgenic seeds causing famines in these nations, and the consequent increase in poverty.

In other words, the supposed enemies of the West, as in this case Vladimir Putin, also share mentors like Henry Kissinger, with Western tycoons like Bill Gates, while they make agreements and help each other in their national causes and businesses. This helps us to see that the supposed enemies of the globalist agenda are not so deep down, but that they take advantage of the globalist agenda for their own purposes and causes, whether national or personal, that is to say that supposed enemies maintain relations of convenience according to their own interests as well.

THE GLOBALIST AGENDA 2.0.

WAR, FOOD AND ENERGY CRISIS.

THE PUTIN-BILL GATES DEAL.

INTRODUCTION

If the pandemic was used to increase social control, advance the world government with the health excuse and destroy the economy with confinements, now a new stage begins in which inflation will serve to implement a new monetary order, but it will be a new dual East-West order, with the eastern side headed by China and Russia, and the western side led by the United States and Europe. This new dual order will not be based on two economic models, since the two economic models of the East and the West are very similar, but rather we are going to experience the fight for world finances, the fight for currency hegemony, with a dollar that its future is being played out by the actions of the White House itself and by the United States Treasury, and the rise of a new monetary standard that in principle was going to be produced in a few years, but that already has an embryo or project, having as protagonist not the yuan, but the ruble and raw materials. The West has the dollar and wants to sink countries with raw materials like Russia.

In the first two books of this series we talked about the fact that the financial, technological and political elites want to impose a New World Order in order to impose a global corporate socialism, that is, a socialism led by some elites together with the large business corporations, where most of the people are poorer, more controlled by this minority elite, and where nation states lose authority becoming mere protectors, in favor of a globalist supranational state or authority.

If in the first two books it was explained about the first part of the globalist agenda 2030 that has been carried out in the year 2020-2021 with the Covid pandemic-plandemic , in order to get used to confinements, to obey, to lose freedoms and to use and share our private digital health data in exchange for supposed health security or any other type, that is, in order to implement digital identities aiming to implement digital currencies issued by Central Banks in the medium term, making money disappear cash; the second part of the 2030 globalist agenda has begun in 2022 with Russia's first attack on Ukraine on February 24, 2022, with the inflation in prices in general and especially that of fuels and food, which was already taking place since the year 2021, the incipient breaks in the supply chains and the famines that are predicted in the short term.

Nothing that happens in this globalist agenda is by chance as we will demonstrate in this book, since Russia's attack on Ukraine had already been predicted by articles in the English magazine owned by the Rothchild banking family, the Economist, specifically the articles of the October 26, 2017, issue on Vladimir Putin, with the cover title "A Tsar is born". This Russian attack on Ukraine had also been communicated, for example, by Henry Kissinger to Bill Gates before 2013, since Kissinger is one of his favorite mentors as well as Putin's.

In addition, the destruction of Russia as an enemy to beat had been published in the report of January 1, 2019, (before the Covid plandemic, or planned pandemic) of the American corporation or "think tank" Rand, entitled "Overextending and unbalancing Russia", which pointed out that it had to be brought to a situation that would hit its gas and oil exports through economic sanctions, while among the steps that had to be taken to achieve it, included the European Union reducing its import of Russian gas, replacing it with liquefied natural gas from the United States. This report also says that Russia's image abroad must be damaged not only through propaganda, but also by prohibiting its participation in sporting events, which is exactly what is happening in 2022 with Russia.

And not only did the current situation of sanctions against Russia appear in the Rand Corporation report, but also in the NATO 2030 report, dated November 25, 2020, in which NATO says it has reached out to Russia to cooperate, and as Putin has rejected it, then NATO has decided to reinforce its forces, raising the need to provide the allies with more nuclear capabilities

On the other hand, the famines that are going to occur in the coming months of 2022 as a result of the food crisis had already been predicted by Henry Kissinger, and in this way Bill Gates has already sold his shares in other sectors and began to buy lands in the United States since 2013, saying that he was doing it because he had been told that a great food crisis would come. For its part, the Economist magazine also released a cover on May 19, 2022, with the title of "The coming food catastrophe" illustrated by three ears of wheat with skulls and articles talking about future famines.

Previously, in October 2015, the Food Chain Reaction drill was officially produced, organized in 2015 by the World Wild Fund (WWF) and John Podesta's Center for American Progress, to analyze the consequences of a great famine that would take place in the period 2020-2030, whose similarities to the current crisis are unsettling and show how globalist elites use these war and hunger games to further their agenda, similar to how the Bill & Melinda Gates Foundation, the World Economic Forum and the John Hopkins University organized the Event 201 in October 2019, just a month and a half before the Covid plandemic broke out, simulating just a corononavirus pandemic .

In this way, the economic sanctions against Russia suppose the beginning of a financial war that the globalist elites want to take advantage of to start the "Great Reset ", as the World Economic Forum calls it. While famines, rationing and energy crises will be used to decimate the population as part of the 2030 globalist agenda, while implanting a new dual monetary system, in which digital currencies and the fight for raw materials will be the protagonists

We will reveal in this book NATO's program to become strong and prepare for a confrontation with China and prevent its rise as the first power. A struggle at an economic, geopolitical, health and digital level in which conventional war has less importance than in other world wars, although as we are seeing in Ukraine, it continues to be the driving force. Destroying Russia, sacrificing Europe using the alleged climate change or global warming caused by humans as an excuse, and setting up a New World Order are the objectives that Western elites want to achieve by 2030.

We will finally see how Bill Gates positioned himself after the fall of the former Soviet Union to establish a Windows monopoly in the new Russia, which he achieved with the help of Putin, who helped authoritatively control Microsoft software piracy, in return that the Kremlin received the operating system from Gates with the excuse of increasing the security of its citizens, but with the real objective of spying on and controlling them.

While in parallel Bill Gates, taking advantage of the artificially created tragedy of the energy and food crisis, built step by step a gigantic food empire thanks to privileged information, among other suppliers, provided by Putin, and with crucial partners that link him both to the Russian and the Ukrainian oligarchy, and to the most intimate surroundings of the Ukrainian president Volodymyr Zelenskyy. Gates began buying land in the United States in 2013, positioning himself as the main landowner in this nation, following the advice of his adviser, the former United States Secretary of State, Henry Kissinger, who stated: "If you control the oil, you control the nations, if you control food, you control people", which received the Nobel Peace Prize in 1973.

In addition Bill Gates with the coalition, Agra, formed by the Bill and Melinda Gates Foundation and the Rockefeller Foundation, for the Green Revolution in Africa, replaced in several African countries the local natural crops for crops with transgenic seeds causing famines in these nations, and the consequent increase in poverty.

In other words, the supposed enemies of the West, as in this case Vladimir Putin, also share mentors like Henry Kissinger, with Western tycoons like Bill Gates, while they make agreements and help each other in their national causes and businesses. This helps us to see that the supposed enemies of the globalist agenda are not so deep down, but that they take advantage of the globalist agenda for their own purposes and causes, whether national or personal, that is to say that supposed enemies maintain relations of convenience according to their own interests as well.

PART ONE: ABOUT THE RUSSIA-UKRAINE WAR

IMMEDIATE GEOPOLITICAL BACKGROUND TO THE RUSSIA-UKRAINE WAR FROM 2021

Europe is only a pawn, but we are told that the joint decision by the European Union to impose economic sanctions on Russia strengthens their union, and that the EU has very quickly agreed as it has not done before in deciding to put these sanctions: in the first hours the European Union already agreed on the sanctions against Russia, which include the blocking of reserves of the Central Bank of Russia, that is, the West has taken away from the Central Bank of Russia its reserves in foreign currency and in gold, which implies sending the message to the world that the money of another nation can be stolen. Imagine going to the bank and not being able to withdraw the money, they tell us that it is confiscated or expropriated, because this would be the same case. In other words, this decision is telling the world that the dollar and the euro are not safe currencies. In the currency battle of the dollar against the ruble since the Russian military intervention, the ruble has regained its value, and it is the euro that is losing its value against the dollar, as BlackRock said back in the day that the euro is dead. By the way, we have all been told that this decision was made after the beginning of the Russian military intervention, but this is not the case, since the decision begins to take shape in November 2021, at which time NATO increases the shipment of weapons to Ukraine, about which very little is said. Thus, the amount of weapons that arrives in Ukraine at the end of 2021 is spectacular, just after Victoria Nuland met with Vladimir Putin to pretend that they did not reach any agreement, that is, to justify the disagreement with the Russian president and begin to say that the Russians were going to attack Ukraine. From then on, the headlines of all the media began to say massively that the Russians were going to invade Ukraine. Then weeks went by and there was no invasion, and in NATO they get nervous, deciding to send more weapons to Ukraine, while telling the Ukrainians to continue attacking the Donbass region of Ukraine. Then the US and British military intelligence begins to leak to the media that Russia's attack on Ukraine will be at the end of January 2022, something that Biden himself goes so far as to verbalize. While in November 2021, Joe Biden asks his Treasury secretary, Janet Yellen , to prepare an economic attack on Russia and to coordinate with the United Kingdom and Europe. That is when the sanctions against Russia begin to be designed. A senior State Department official has confirmed to the Financial Times that between the time Biden asks Janet Yellen to prepare an economic attack on Russia, and the Russian military intervention in Ukraine on February 24, 2022, senior officials from the Biden administration spent an average of 10 to 15 hours a week in secure calls or video conferences with the European Union and member states to coordinate sanctions on a military intervention that had not taken place, and in fact had been taking a long time saying that it was going to happen, while weapons were being sent to Ukraine and people from Eastern Ukraine were being killed, favoring and promoting a civil war. In Washington, United States, the sanctions plans were led by a man named Daleep Singh, who is a former New York Federal Reserve official, who is deputy national security adviser for the international economy in the White House, who he also worked in the Obama administration. While the person in charge on the part of the European Union was the chief of staff of the president of the European Commission, Úrsula Von der Leyer, Mr. Bjoern Seibert , who works for NATO associated with the Massachusetts Institute of Technology (MIT), and who has a close relationship with the US military-industrial complex, for whom he has worked most of his life. So in the European Union when they were voting on that famous law to avoid opening the Nord Stream 2 gas pipeline, they thought they were voting on something that had already been decided. In fact, it was already decided by the intelligence of the United Kingdom, the intelligence of the United States, and a man from NATO was negotiating, that is, from the United States military complex. In this way, this trio designs a strategy that must begin with forcing Germany not to open the new gas pipeline built with Russia, Nord Stream 2, which was going to increase the shipment of Russian gas to Europe, and which according to the Rand report Corporation , the United States considered that it was the beginning of a Eurasian union, and that was what the US Pentagon wanted to avoid at all costs. In this way, the role of Ukraine was directly ended, since it would not be a country of passage for gas pipelines and robbery, its role in this globalist NATO (NATO) agenda disappeared . According to the same State Department official consulted by the Financial Times, it is considered that not opening this gas pipeline would be a very important signal to other Europeans that sacred cows had to be sacrificed. In this case the sacred cow of Germany is sacrificed. In fact, German politicians said that they had never had such close security contacts with the Americans in history as they do now.

Then comes the blockade of the reserves of the Russian Central Bank, which does not come from the United States or the United Kingdom but rather from Canada. In this way blocking the reserves of the Central Bank of Russia is the Minister of Finance of Canada Chrystia Freeland , who is of Ukrainian descent and has been in contact with Kiev officials for many years, is also the woman who decided to act against the truckers by freezing their bank accounts. It's funny that this woman is called Chrystia

Freeland , because Christian doesn't seem to have much and Freeland (means "free land" in Spanish) doesn't seem to have much either; although this name and surnames have been given by her as usually happens when someone becomes a US citizen, and they are not her original name and surname. Similarly , Victoria Nuland , who is an American diplomat, also comes from a family of Ukrainian Jews, so there are a lot of people who are along these lines. A few hours after Russian tanks began pouring into Ukraine, Chrystia Freeland sends a written proposal to the United States Treasury and the United States Department of State, that is, he sends a letter to Janet Yellen saying what they were going to do: punish the Russian Central Bank. That day Trudeau, Prime Minister of Canada and maximum exponent of the globalist agenda goes to the G7 summit, and also says that they are going to punish the Russian Central Bank. Mrs. Freeland , before being a senior official in the Canadian government, was editor of the Financial Times newspaper, was editor of the Reuters news agency and is a woman very close to George Soros, even considering her Soros's journalist. in fact Freeland has carefully interviewed Soros many times.

in fact Freeland has carefully interviewed Soros many times. In fact Chrystia Freeland has just approved a rule with which they can take away people's savings from the bank, that is, it is she herself who is initiating that monetary reset. In this way, in an interview that Freeland did with George Soros in 2015, he clearly says that the European Union is doomed and that it should advance in the globalist project. With the G7 Freeland project, the European Emergency Summit is held on the night of February 24, 2022, with Mario Draghi taking command, who has served as Italian Prime Minister since 2021 and was president of the European Central Bank from 2011 until in 2019. In theory they put him as Prime Minister of Italy to save Italy from the crisis, and of course they put him to vaccinate the entire population of Italy, which was the first thing he said he was going to do. Possibly they also put Mario Draghi as Prime Minister of Italy to lead that

European Union, a character who has largely brought us to the inflationary situation that we have now and the visible head of that dark group of 30, an organization that we talked about in the second part of this series on the Globalist Agenda, and which directs global monetary policy, being the Central Bank of the world government, being above the BIS (Bank for International Settlements), that is, the Bank for International Settlements. By the way, both the group of 30 and the Bank for International Settlements have a website.

RAND CORPORATION REPORT JANUARY 1, 2019: OVEREXTENDING AND UNBALANCED RUSSIA

Several years ago the current Ukraine crisis was planned. The first, on October 1, 1945, the United States Armed Forces created the Rand project, an acronym for Research and Development , that is, research and development through a special contract signed with the Douglas Aircraft Company. It was, therefore, a clear manifestation of the activities of the military industrial complex that would bother President Howard. Subsequently, the Rand Corporation began operations in December 1945, and by the end of 1947 that project became a separate organization from Douglas Aircraft in February 1948. The chief of staff of the newly created United States Air Force wrote a letter to President of the Douglas Aircraft Company, which approved the evolution of the Rand project into a non-profit corporation independent of Douglas

Subsequently on May 14, 1948, Rand was registered as a not-for-profit company under the laws of the State of California, and

on November 1 of 1948, the contract for the Rand project was formally transferred from the Douglas Aircraft Company to the Rand Corporation. The fact that it became a non-profit entity allowed Rand to receive enormous amounts of money without paying a single dollar in taxes.

Although the Rand Corporation is presented as an independent entity and is certainly private in its management, its financing depends mostly on the Department of Defense of the Department of Homeland Security of the United States, and other government departments, as well as different universities and private entities. .

With some 2,000 employees, more than half of whom have doctorates in their field, Rand produces policy reports and plans in areas such as international politics, energy and education, recruited from more than 50 countries each year. Rand's employees speak 75 languages and are spread across offices and sub-sites in the United States, Europe, Australia and the Persian Gulf region. The Rand Corporation has US personnel in more than 25 countries.

During the 1950s, Rand developed the thesis of nuclear deterrence through mutually assured destruction. This thesis was developed under the guidance of then Secretary of Defense Robert Magnamara , and was based on work with game theory under the auspices of John Von Neumann. Significantly, Rand's chief strategist, German Khan, also floated the idea of a nuclear exchange in which the Soviet Union could be beaten. Khan would appear portrayed in the movie "Red Telephone. We fly to Moscow", by Stanley Kubrick as Doctor Strangelove , responsible for a nuclear Holocaust. In that same film, Rand appeared, but as Black society.

Rand has contributed to programs such as those related to the space race, computer science, artificial intelligence and the so-called war games. However, its influence is also considerable in areas such as child policy, health, international politics, intelligence, the arts or crisis management, among others. Still, roughly half of Rand's activity is directly related to national security.

On January 1, 2019, that is, now more than 3 years ago, Rand published a strategic plan specifically directed against Russia and entitled " Overextending and unbalancing Russia ". That is, " Overextending and unbalancing Russia." The text was signed by James Dobbins , Raphael S. Cohen, Nathan Chandler, Bryan Frederick, Edward Geist, Paul DeLuca , Forrest E. Morgan, Howard J. Shatz, and Brent Williams, and was published in May 2019. This plan stated Its objective was to provoke an overextension of Russia that would allow its imbalance and with it its destruction.

In order to destroy Russia, the plan drawn up by Rand 3 years ago indicated that it had to be brought to a situation that would hit its gas and oil exports through economic sanctions, among the steps that had to be taken to achieve this, it included that the European Union reduce its import of Russian gas, replacing it with liquefied natural gas from the United States.

Along with these economic measures aimed at harming Russia, the Rand document pointed out that the image of Russia abroad must be harmed through propaganda, or only by giving a negative image, but also by ensuring, for example, that it be excluded from the sports events.

At the same time, it was necessary, according to Rand, that NATO member nations be pressured to increase their military budget and direct it expressly against Russia.

This plan, elaborated by Rand, presented enormous advantages, since in addition to economic gains, the United States would reduce its military spending, focusing mainly on strategic bombers and long-range missiles directed against Russia. While the deployment in Europe of new intermediate-range nuclear missiles implied, according to Rand, enormous probabilities of success and the risk, of course, not small, it would only be borne by European nations.

Within this strategy of destroying Russia, Ukraine had to play an essential role and in fact, in 2019, in the aforementioned plan, Rand stated that providing Ukraine with lethal aid would exploit Russia's most important point of external weakness, but Any increase in arms and military advice that the United States provides to Ukraine will have to be methodically calibrated to impose costs on Russia, without provoking a much broader conflict in which Russia, given its proximity, would have significant advantages. In other words, Ukraine, considered Russia's most important point of external weakness, should be armed.

The extent to which NATO has been arming Ukraine as a way of harming Russia, the Rand project pointed out, can be inferred not only from the dozens of biochemical weapons laboratories established on Ukrainian soil, but also from the more than 2,000 structures destroyed so far by Russia, and actually built and controlled not by Ukrainian nationalists, but by the US and NATO commanders. This immense military structure makes it necessary to consider whether the information about Zelensky's construction of a dirty nuclear bomb can tragically correspond to reality.

The Rand plan excludes any attempt at a peaceful and diplomatic settlement of the situation, which would explain the rejection of all Russia's negotiation proposals formulated during the first months of 2022, and would also explain the refusal to offer guarantees not to expand the NATO, since NATO is a key player in the growing harassment directed against a Russia that must be destroyed. If one were to believe the insistent war propaganda, but in reality also very crude and directed at an ignorant public with which the West has been hammering away for months, the current conflict in Ukraine would be a struggle between good and evil, between light and darkness, between democracy and totalitarianism. In this way, the despotic and cruel Russia would be attacking the beautiful and free Ukraine, moved by a perverse desire for world domination.

The truth is totally different for various agendas that add the American unipolar hegemony plan to the globalist agenda. Russia is an enemy that must be beaten and destroyed. The causes of that decision are far from the defense of freedom, nor international security, nor even the interests of the West. In reality, they are reduced to the search for power and the desire to displace Russia from markets like the European ones, from gas and oil. This attack against Russia would have to be subsequently dismembered and looted, as happened in the 90s of the last century.

All these plans have as their stage and main victims the nations that are located on the European continent. It is Europe that has to bear astronomical economic losses from losing access to Russian energy, and being forced to buy American gas, which is much more expensive.

It is Europe that has to make the greatest military expenditures, not really for its own benefit, but to threaten a nation like Russia, with which it would be very interested in maintaining excellent relations. It is Europe that will host the deployment of the largest nuclear weapons, assuming of course the blow of suffering an atomic war. And it is Europe that will lose all its political and economic independence to the benefit of powerful extra-European lobbies. Within this strategy of harassment, encirclement and destruction of Russia, the key piece is Ukraine, and it is not because it is intended to defend it, but because it constitutes the ideal platform to destroy Russia from its territory.

Pentagon and NATO military installations make it clear that Ukraine does not belong to the Ukrainians, and that its corrupt oligarchs to the core bend against national interests at the will of foreign powers, even at the cost of gravely risking the peace and tranquility of the Ukrainians.

The fact that successive Ukrainian governments have allowed the location of hundreds of foreign military installations, including several dozen biochemical weapons laboratories on their territory, makes it clear that although they are worshipers of the genocidal Stepan Bandera, that although they may have Nazi units in their Army , as is the case, among others of the Azov battalion, but they are still mere servile lackeys of strategies conceived thousands of kilometers from their land, after all, as the Rand document points out, Ukraine is the key piece to try to annihilate Russia.

All in all, and despite the fact that Europe is and will be the one that will suffer the most from the consequences of the plans exposed by Rand three years ago, the people of the United States will not emerge unscathed from the ambitions of their monopolar and globalist elites. The inflation that cannot be controlled, the submission to propaganda aimed at justifying wars without any justification, the increase in military spending that already accounts for 53% of the national budget, the growing international contempt for maneuvers of economic and political submission difficult to hide, and the tributes paid in blood and in social neglect will not be paid by George Soros, Bill Gates, the Biden family or even the members of Rand will be assumed one hundred percent by the American people.

Despite all the conspiracies that seek to justify wars and foreign interventions often fail, and end up being discovered sooner or later with dire consequences. When this happens, the results are not as expected and the existence of a hidden, although undeniable, cosmic justice can be glimpsed.

NATO REPORT 2030

The final report is dated November 25, 2020 and is only available in English under the title "NATO 2030: United for a new era." Analysis and recommendations of the reflection group appointed by the Secretary General of NATO. The original English title is: NATO 2030: United for a new era. Analysis and recommendations of the reflection group appointed by the NATO secretary general.

This report proposes that NATO be the new world government without using this term. For NATO, only the West matters and not the rest of the world, no matter how inclusive they want to call themselves.

In fact, it is very revealing to see how the beginning of this new, it is just December 2019 when the Covid plan began, to apply this global control strategy to apply it in the following decade 2020-2030. In this report, NATO justifies its existence because after the fall of the USSR, NATO has no reason to exist and how later more or less democratic countries were formed in the USSR and in Europe, but since in reality the aims of NATO are different.

NATO justifies its existence for 2030 based on 5 axes:

Russia, China, Isis terrorism, the digitalization of the world and climate change.

In this new era Russia is the enemy of the world so that once on its knees, integrating it into the organization. use it as a vassal by necessarily collaborating with NATO. NATO justifies this role by saying that it has extended its hand to Putin, he has rejected it, and they mark the annexation of Crimea in 2014 as a key date, eluding once again that the annexation of Crimea follows the coup in Ukraine , and that the annexation of Ukraine came after elections, after NATO designed and executed a coup in Ukraine, which led to a civil war.

This document is public, and is used as a basis for indoctrination, in which NATO boasts of the invasion of Yugoslavia in the 90s and of Libya. He says he has reached out to Russia to cooperate, and since Putin has said no, he has decided to reinforce NATO forces, raising the need to provide the allies with more nuclear capabilities . Calls for the deployment in Europe of the new B6112 nuclear bombs and new intermediate-range nuclear missiles to be speeded up. In this way, Russia is forced to perhaps send some nuclear bomb or missile and thus NATO has an excuse to attack Russia.

Should Russia attack, the devastating effects of Russian bombs or missiles would be borne by Ukraine or Europe and not by the United States, which become mere expendable instruments of NATO.

China is the second axis that would justify the existence of NATO according to this document. In this way, the analysts of the Atlantic alliance assume as their own the prophecy of the World Economic Forum that China will be the world leader in the year 2030, and according to this report it does not seem that they aspire to avoid it. Thus, while in this document they are very belligerent with Russia and think that they will defend themselves with all their means against NATO attacks, with respect to China they say that many things unite them, because possibly the elites of the globalist agenda trust that the The Chinese will lure them onto their turf, because they're partially dumb, so you're having a racist analysis of the Chinese. It is hoped that the Chinese Communist Party is as corrupt as the Russian Communist Party was, and can be dominated as Boris Yeltsin was dominated, but the truth is that the Chinese are even more dangerous, nationalistic, and look with more contempt on the West than what the Russians do.

There is also a mistake in thinking that the Chinese Communist

Party is like the Soviet Communist Party of the 1990s, and that they are going to absorb China into the globalist agenda and control them.

Thus, the economic sanctions against China are not even mentioned because they would mainly affect the United States but also Europe, while the economic sanctions against Russia mainly affect Europe. Then there is talk of blowing up the foundations of the new Chinese silk road, a route from Europe to Southeast Asia connected by land and sea and with commercial relations.

In fact, the Alliance is aware that the allied countries maintain close economic, commercial and supply relations with vital products for the industry, as has been seen in the crisis in the first half of 2022, so a radical rupture is not considered. but the importance of making a common front and not reaching agreements that could produce an increase in this dependence on China.

The truth is that there is also a certain impotence behind this , because the only thing that is clearly intended is to control the information that is provided to the West so that no one considers alternatives to the globalist leadership of NATO, saying that this is an operation of the Chinese, which is false because the West is not being censored by the Chinese.

It seems that the idea is to end up courting the Chinese, which is that idea of sharing the world that is present in a part of those Western elites, referring to the fact that John Hopkins University released a report saying that the relationship between the United States and China is like two strands of DNA, one red and one blue. So it seems that the report says that for now we are going to deal with Russia and in 2030 maybe with a bit of luck we have convinced the Chinese.

Within this plan, NATO also calls for the creation of an agency for advanced European defense projects that is equivalent to DARPA (Defense advanced Research Projects Agency), which translated into Spanish would be the United States Defense Advanced

Research Projects Agency, which creates many technologies and projects that will be used in society in the next 20-30 years. In addition, in Europe there are not so many legal and administrative limitations to test these projects, especially Eastern European countries, and they can even use facilities that are already built.

Regarding axis 3, that is, climate change, NATO intends to use it not to protect nature or so that there is less pollution, but because it fears that the melting of the Arctic will leave the ground clear for Russia to exploit and extract fossil fuels. or hydrocarbons, and lately the Russians are not standing still in the Arctic. And now that hydrocarbons are the protagonists, and the Arctic is a source of fishing, tariffs can be applied to access there, that is, a lot of money can be obtained from there.

In fact, the Arctic contains 22% of the world's hydrocarbon reserves, and it also has other raw materials, precious stones, metals, gold, silver, copper, iron, lead, magnesium, nickel, platinum, etc., although even more What is important are the possibilities that the Arctic routes bring to global maritime trade, which are going to change everything in maritime transport, because the distances are going to be much shorter, a lot of time is going to be saved, fuel is going to be saved, which is one of the keys also currently, and the risk of piracy that exists in the Indian routes is avoided, which is one of the biggest problems at the moment.

At the moment it is still dangerous to navigate between ice at certain times of the year, but technology and the melting in the north are advancing, and it is a matter of time before this new route is opened at the same time that the seasonal window is extended in which it can be browse. By the way, this is the only thing NATO seems to be interested in about climate change, while they continually talk about CO_2. They also don't care that the biggest problem that nature now has is pollution of rivers, since they there is no talk or emission rights.

The last axis around which the NATO agenda is articulated is that of terrorism. NATO mentions ISIS in this document, but considering it as the only global terrorist threat is not true, knowing that Isis, Daesh or Islamic State was created by the US CIA, with the weapons supply and training program of terrorists of the year 2012, by the intelligence services of Arab countries, headed by the intelligence services of Saudi Arabia , in what is known as Operation Timber Sycamore created to overthrow President Bashar Arafat of the Syrian Arab Republic. In this operation of which there are even photographs of how the Daesh were taught to shoot, the Saudis put the money and the CIA provided the rest of the means .

This is a summary of NATO's plan for the year 2030, at least in its geopolitical aspect , which is an action of the globalist agenda, which has the Ukraine conflict as its great catalyst. In this way, since Joe Biden became president of the United States, the focus has been on two points, one in Eastern Europe with Ukraine as the protagonist, and in the Pacific with an eye on Taiwan, in which there was a small crisis, and that it is a fundamental country for producing semiconductors to build these new societies, smart cities or prisons with digital identifications.

Russia's invasion of Ukraine was preceded by an increase in Zelensky's attacks on Donbass residents. In fact there was shelling of civilians in the Donbas the weekend before the Russian attack on Ukraine. It was a matter of time before Russia's intervention in Ukraine took place, since in 2014 a civil war began in Ukraine, and it seems as if NATO was anticipating a scenario that would occur later in the future.

NATO in this report intends to form a New World Order with two hermetic blocks. It is a new order that is currently taking place and that implies sacrificing Europe, ending German industry by forcing the so-called ecological transition to be accelerated, increasing dependence on US gas, directing the digitalization of the economy to increase social control under the NATO cloak. It is no coincidence that before the Russian intervention in Ukraine, the European Union decided to include gas in the taxonomy of green and sustainable energies. Why? Because now Europe is going to have to consume the green and sustainable liquefied gas from the United States, which is 40% more expensive than Russian gas.

This is consistent with a White House plan that seeks to integrate the military-industrial complex with health warfare and biological warfare, to use this new Pentagon capability to direct the energy system by monopolizing the energy storage system, batteries that need rare earths to be produced, which are found especially in China and Russia, so there are going to be conflicts in the Pacific.

SECOND PART: ABOUT THE FOOD AND ENERGY CRISIS

THE MANUFACTURED GREAT FAMINE TO EXPAND THE GLOBALIST AGENDA

Another phenomenon that was already beginning to take place before the arrival of the Ukraine War, which showed its face with the pandemic and which is now being catalyzed by Western sanctions on Russia, like so many other elements of the globalist agenda, is the great famine. that is going to take place in the coming months and that, in addition to economic explanations, has a lot to do with this Great Restart project, or Great Reset, as the World Economic Forum calls it.

In fact, in recent years China has managed to lift more than 800 million people out of poverty, and poverty has also been greatly reduced in India, which are the two most populous nations on the planet, and therefore hunger was about to be eradicated as a problem in the world.

The planet's food supply works with a 90-day cycle, so any obstruction in that present or future cycle then influences the lack of food. But they are saying that this is because of the war in Ukraine, while the truth is that technology already makes it easy for anyone to go without food, and natural food, not printed food.

Another problem is the huge increase in the price of fertilizers, of which Russia is precisely one of the largest manufacturers because Russia is rich in phosphorus (in fact, Western Sahara has one of the largest reserves of phosphorus in the world, and for this reason Morocco and The United States were very interested in Western Sahara becoming Moroccan domain and not Spanish), nitrogen and potassium and other minerals necessary to produce them. Fertilizers are obviously essential to ensure good crop growth. In fact , approximately 50% of world food production depends on fertilizers, and precisely Russia is a nation in the production of the compounds that make up fertilizers .

Nitrogen is produced mainly with natural gas, which has tripled in price in recent months. 10% of the phosphorus also comes from Russia and this nation is also the second largest exporter of potassium on the planet, being also a power in the production of fertilizers, although its government is increasingly globalist and repressive, see the example of economic sanctions against the truck drivers who went on strike for not wanting to be vaccinated.

For her part , Chrystia Freeland , this lady who is a friend of Soros, designed those sanctions or at least is the one who puts them on paper, which is precisely what causes countries to not be able to buy those fertilizers. She is precisely of Ukrainian origin, and these fertilizers are necessary for agricultural activity, that is, in this case we can assure that it is, at least in this aspect, a created or manufactured crisis.

The Foreign Agricultural Service of the US Department of Agriculture has made a report to study the repercussion of the war in Ukraine on the production and distribution of grain, as well as the repercussion that this war has on the agricultural sector. In this report, which can be downloaded in English under the title "The Ukraine conflict and other factors contributing to high commodities prices and food insecurity " (The Ukraine conflict and other factors contributing to high commodity prices and food insecurity), have essentially said that the war was the last nail in the coffin that had been building for a long time.

Specifically, this report was carried out to gauge the impact of the war in Ukraine on this lower supply of food and grain, and fundamentally it shows that there are other elements that matter more than the war in Ukraine, such as the imposition of prohibitions and restrictions on exports by countries, something that is not new, but precisely the European Union has been founded on these 2 pillars. It is basically preventing farmers from being able to produce freely, and instead they are subsidized and "helped" by governments.

The increase in energy costs, as a result of the reckless commitment to renewable energies, as the only source of energy, also has a great impact on agricultural and grain production. Another factor that influences the supply of agricultural production is the natural weather conditions themselves, obviously those who proclaim climate change due to human action, attributing all the blame to human beings. How powerful the human being that can even cause droughts!

The scarcity of grain and agricultural supply is also influenced by the incredible increase in global demand, led by China. But it is that the reduction of poverty and of the human beings who go hungry, which has occurred in recent decades, is largely attributed to Chinese development. It has a very simple one and it also has an explanation linked to the East, because China has gone from an agricultural economy to a service economy or is going to a service economy in almost the blink of an eye. Obviously China still has a high industrial component, but China is the big buyer. If we look at the graphs and tables of the Agricultural Department, we can see to what extent the Government and Chinese companies have made supply a State policy, since it was known that Ukraine was a powder keg after the coup of the Euro Maidan in 2014 perpetrated by NATO.

If you look at the charts in the US Department of Agriculture reports from 2016 onwards, Russia and China are stocking up by buying gold and food. In fact, in Russia, in addition to weapons, they have bought gold and food. So there is no doubt that

Russian and Chinese politicians are not only politicians but also statesmen, which is not the case with Western politicians. Being statesmen, they are people who plan for many years because they saw the scarcity of agricultural supply and famines coming, like Bill Gates. In addition, in the West what has been done at the same time is to bring down the market, when the Chinese were criticized saying that they had no market.

In fact, the market is the one that serves to solve these problems, adjusting the offer to a greater demand. In other words, if there is a very large increase in demand, not only for the reasons that we are commenting on, but because after the Covid plan , and after the confinements, there is a brutal explosion in demand, also financed by central banks, and precisely adjusting supply takes time, but it can only be done if there are no bureaucratic obstacles, and if supply is not adjusted on time, prices skyrocket, especially with each political intervention it grows higher. Every decision that is made in any field, the only thing that does is raise the price of energy, and although the rise in prices increases the incentives to produce more, for there to be more harvests, this price rise has to be produced without there being excessive bureaucratic obstacles, and then the law of supply and demand would be put to work correctly. In other words, farmers would go to work attracted by high prices because that is how the market works. Let them tell the people about the extraction of oil through the energy of fracking, for example. In this way the offer would be adjusted, but this cannot happen because precisely the agricultural sector is one of the most intervened in the world, and in the countries where it is not so intervened because there are no important legal structures, the State is the first thing that What he does is intervene in the agricultural sector thinking about self-consumption, which is a big mistake, since each one has to produce what has a comparative advantage, and let the others work and sell.

Some can, for example, make bananas, other apples, but each one must specialize in what they know how to do best and at the lowest price, and if there are no bureaucratic obstacles, we are allowed to create an industry. For example, maybe we created the industry to treat the banana and put it in cans and sell it, and maybe we need a specific technology to harvest that banana and we have it. To produce more and better, innovation is necessary, while when social engineers, businessmen and state politicians get their hands dirty, they kill those local producers that they claimed to defend, who are currently having a very bad time

In short, Russia and China have prepared in advance for a famine situation as revealed by the reports of the United States Department of Agriculture, such as the one that is expected to arrive soon, while the Western countries have not done so, because their governments do not they look after the interests of their countries and citizens, but rather to comply with the plans and objectives of the globalist agenda of the New World Order.

PROPHECY OF FAMINE IN 2020-2030. CHAIN FOOD REACTION SIMULATION. YEAR 2015.

The Food Simulacrum Chain Reaction , organized in 2015 by the World Wild Fund , WWF, or World Wide Fund for Nature translated into Spanish, and John Podesta 's Center for American Progress analyzed the consequences of a great famine that would take place in the period 2020-2030. The similarities with the current crisis are disturbing and show how globalist elites use these war games to implement their agenda.

In fact, whenever we see who the creators and organizers are, we always find the same people and organizations that want to implement a New World Order based on the Great Globalist Reset and with the 2030 agenda.

So when we talk about famines we are reminded of the cover of the British magazine The Economist of May 19, 2022, with a headline that reads: " The coming food catastrophe ", or in Spanish the food crisis that is coming, with three ears of wheat that instead of grains have skulls, and attributing to Putin and Russia the death of millions of people from hunger.

In these drills organized by the globalist elites, which later always become a reality, such as event 201, which on October 18, 2019, was organized by John Hopkins University together with the Bill and Melinda Gates Foundation, to act worldwide against an alleged coronavirus pandemic that a month and a half later became a reality, some instructions are given, a series of manuals, which are the instructions that are presented in globalist organizations such as the Bilderberg Club, the Trilateral Commission, the Council on International Relations, etc. .

Thus, on November 9 and 10, 2015, 65 political leaders, business executives, scientists and social researchers with deep experience working on food and agricultural issues make up 8 teams and meet at the headquarters of the World Wide Fund , WWF, which is the organization whose symbol is a panda bear, whose official objective is the conservation of nature, but which in reality is one more arm of the octopus created by the Club of Rome, to implement the Malthusian green agenda.

The WWF are very good at bringing in money and they have their headquarters in Switzerland, which is where Klaus Schwab, founder of the World Economic Forum, has an NGO in Geneva, and where the face-to-face meetings of this Forum take place, that is, in Davos, Swiss.

The WWF has been accused of financing, equipping and collaborating with paramilitary forces. According to Buzzfeed ,

WWF has operated as a global espionage center by organizing, financing and managing dangerous and secret networks of whistleblowers, motivated by fear and thirst for revenge in indigenous communities, in order to provide confidential information to the addresses of the parks while publicly denying working with the informant.

The pretend game was called Food Chain Reaction , Food Chain Reaction in Spanish, and its organizers said that it was a simulation to provide information and help us prepare for the future, or in the words of the designers themselves for a "new normality". Yes, in 2015 people began to talk about "new normality" or "new normal" in English, which is the phrase that we would constantly hear from all politicians from 2020 with the Covid plandemic . In fact, the term new normal appears in the reports several times, while the organizers themselves call it a world food security game, in which the participants play a role, that is, it is like a role-playing game, and in this way explore how they might respond during a future crisis in the global food system, in this case a major famine

Attendees were presented with a future scenario, precisely the year 2020, and told that they would be in a world where population growth, rapid urbanization, extreme weather and political crises combine to create a huge famine, which is what we are beginning to see in this second half of the year 2022, since the energy crisis and increases in fuel prices, among other causes, always cause food crises.

In addition, in this simulation of the Hunger Games, a map of the countries and regions that would have political conflicts in the year 2020 was presented, and precisely Ukraine already appeared in red as a country that would be in conflict, and African countries such as Somalia, which the United States United has invaded in early June 2022.

In fact, the period of this simulation represented a decade, specifically from the year 2020 to 2030, and those attending these Hunger Games for two days collaborated , negotiated, made decisions and faced the consequences of their actions in a given period, in his case it was a decade from the year 2020 to the year 2030. As a play or role playing game it lasted 2 days run by the panda bear World Wild Fund, but with more companions who will be the hard core, more some participants who were senior officials and subject matter experts from teams representing Brazil, mainland Africa, China, the European Union, India, the United States and then multilateral institutions , such as the World Bank and companies and investors, as well as two news agencies Reuters and Bloomberg. Once everyone was seated in their seats in groups, it was explained to them that it is the year 2020 and that in the last five years since 2015, demographic changes, climate pressures, political crises had threatened global security and, therefore, food safety. In the first round of the game, which spanned the years 2020 and 2021, global food stocks were well below average, and prices soared, weather and war catastrophes occurred, and there were instances of civil unrest. The game begins with a plenary session with a video projecting the state of the world in the year 2020.

Attendees were shown a video on arrival, and at the end of the first round the team had to record their key decisions and actions on an informative presentation template. For whom? For those who were watching, that is to say for the Watchers. In this way, the teams delivered their copy to an adjudication cell for review, which is totalitarian because they did not leave the teams freedom in the background. In other words, these gentlemen analyzed everyone's decisions, and then presented them with great alternative scenarios, that is, what is called social engineering. This process is repeated at the end of the 4 rounds.

The second to fourth rounds begin with the determination of the new normality. From the year 2022, the new normality or the updated state of the world would arrive. In the second round spanning 2022 to 2024, players experience the peak of the food safety crisis in the game. That is, significant droughts spread across large production areas, oil prices increase dramatically, reinforcing biofuel production, unrest and migration intensity, food prices rise from 262 to 395% of average values at long term etc. just the same thing that is happening in the year 2022.

Later, little by little, this situation improves in the third round that runs from 2025 to 2027, with a generalized recovery in crop production, a global food program with more money, a renewed focus on climate change and food in the long term, food prices fall from 395 to 141% of the long-term average values.

The fourth round covers the years 2028-2030 with droughts in Brazil, China and the United States, a weak monsoon and civil unrest in India, protests in West African cities, and prices rise again from 141% to 387%. % of long-term mean values.

Later the year 2030 arrives and the situation is already very bad, and a global government is needed to control everything and help us get out of this situation. Does It sound familiar to you?.

In this document of this simulation it is said that the teams agreed to avoid bilateral Community trade agreements, opting instead to engage in broader global partnerships, because long-term solutions require better governance, a world government. And how is this? How do we make a world government? With a real-time security dashboard that enables decision-makers in the public and private sectors to detect and address food system disruptions, which requires hiring a trusted global agent to collect and maintain the data transparently. And here comes social control, since it is necessary to monitor purchases, production in each of the countries, consumption in order to direct it from above. The approach requires countries to transparently report on their food stock, agricultural and food subsidies, land-leasing relationships, and efforts to reduce agriculture-related emissions. In this way the tax on CO2 or there will be taxes on meat due to farting from cows because they expel methane, which creates global warming.

All this according to what will help food producers to plan future production in the face of climatic impacts, that is to say what has happened all life, that farmers cannot control the climate. In this sense, chemtrails , or cloud trails left by planes spraying chemicals in the sky, could have, among other intentions, modify the climate to move agriculture from one place to another.

the Center for American Progress was also present and organized this simulation , which is one of the thinkers most influential tanks or laboratory of ideas in tune with the Clinton and Obama era, especially in the Obama era. Especially in Obama 's with Joe Biden as Vice President. In this way, the president and founder, John Podesta , was responsible for Hillary Clinton's presidential campaign in 2016, whose emails were published by Wikileaks about the Pizza Gate scandal, which has raised all kinds of information and misinformation far and wide. of the network. John Podesta moves freely around the UN, and his think tank is a tool of the United States military-industrial complex because it has businesses, arms companies.

Also when we go to the technical report to check who is that hard core of these hunger games, the adjudication cell and the control group we see that it is made up of four people. One is John Podesta directly, that is, it is not that he put the think tank , it was him. Sitting next to him at this control table is Democratic Senator Tom Daschle . Former intelligence officer, whose wife has worked for the Federal Aviation Administration with the Clinton Administration. His wife worked for top Washington lobbyists with ties to companies like American Airlines, Lock Heed Martin, Boeing. This gentleman has a consulting firm, which, as he indicates on his own website, is a boutique full-service strategic advisory firm with great scope. He was one of Joe Biden 's henchmen by the way.

Also on this event management team was Alan Bierga of Bloomberg News, and one had advanced and a recently deceased lady named Mary Kate Fisher on behalf of the CNA, which is an independent research and analysis organization, and in theory not for profit. dedicated to the security of For 80 years, they say on their website, our scientific rigor and real-world approach to data have been indispensable to leaders facing complex problems. That is pure deep state.

Among the organizations that organized the event were the Albright Stonebridge Group, the consultant of Madeleine Albright, now deceased, Secretary of State of the United States in her day, responsible for massacres in different wars, who justified in interviews the deaths of half a million children in the Iraq war.

He also organized the Chain Food Reaction, Agra, the famous Alliance for a Green Revolution in Africa, the Bill and Melinda Gates Foundation and the Rockefeller Foundation, which with the excuse of climate change forced Third World farmers to buy seeds and fertilizers, which friends of these false philanthropists sold them, borrowing up to the eyebrows, while most of them went bankrupt. And where there have been Agra programs, hunger has increased exponentially because in theory their goal was to reduce hunger but they caused just the opposite.

Gates has in fact always been obsessed with the subject of food and was the first person to start a seed bank many years ago.

And to close this dark circle we have as organizer and collaborator of these Hunger Games, Chain Food Reaction, to the Soros Open Society for a change, which is the George Soros Foundation, to advance the globalist agenda and launder money with the humanitarian excuse.

PART THREE: THE PUTIN AND BILL GATES DEALS, THE RUSSIAN AND UKRAINIAN OLIGARCHIES AND THE WESTERN ELITES. ITS INFLUENCE ON THE WAR AND FOOD AND ENERGY CRISIS.

THIRD PART: THE PUTIN AND BILL GATES DEALS, OLIGARCHIES AND ITS INFLUENCE ON THE WAR AND ON THE FOOD, ENERGY CRISIS

THE SECRET DEAL BETWEEN PUTIN AND BILL GATES.

ITS INFLUENCE ON THE CURRENT WAR AND FOOD CRISIS.

With this fascinating story, the investment route of an expert in surfing waves generated by storms, that is, Bill Gates, is told below with a sum of realities that are not talked about so much about him or the person of Vladimir Putin.

We will also tell about the Western political class, from the United States to the African, from the Mexican to the Spanish, from the Argentine to the British, and the most important thing is that it gives us a precise dimension of the turbulent economic future that lies ahead, especially in the energy plan, which includes the electricity of the fuel and in the food plan.

Bill Gates is profiting from the ruin of millions, not because he is particularly astute and the rest of us are the opposite, but because he has become the most skillful social architect of our time, a gentleman capable of designing, planning and concretizing meticulously determining changes in the political and economic structure of all our countries, from the particular situation that the world is going through as of the year 2020.

We could say that Bill Gates is also a full-fledged progressive activist, but today we have to address another facet, namely his neat investment strategy very much around the conflict in Eastern Europe between Russia and Ukraine. Bill Gates is established as one of the main winners in terms of profits and his particular movements say a lot about the ferocious economic crisis that is beginning to spread like a shock wave to all corners of the planet. Of course, how could it be otherwise, in this tragic scenario there is also a script , a previous roadmap where the American tycoon wrote some of his darkest episodes.

As is public knowledge, since February 2022 Russian troops ruthlessly raze Ukrainian homes leaving houses on fire, civilians executed in the streets, bombing children's hospitals, while Putin and Zelensky set up humanitarian corridors to later destroy them, generating panic in millions of people stranded at its mercy, with carefully calculated attacks like the one Russia perpetrated against the Zaporizhia nuclear plant in early March 2022.

Thus , after the deep collective trauma of the Chernobyl nuclear plant disaster suffered in Ukraine in April 1986, the Russian army tries to force the Ukrainians to surrender unconditionally. However, they have not succeeded, despite the fact that cities like Mariupol are enduring a siege that recalls the dark millennium of feudal communism in the Middle Ages, with no food, water or medicine. The few elderly who survive do so praying on their knees for the survival of the younger ones, while the children faint from dehydration under the rubble of horror. The incessant attack on towns and cities has caused one of the biggest refugee crises of the 21st century, with more than 2.5 million expatriate Ukrainians who are being distributed disorderly throughout the rest of the old continent, increasingly threatened by the Russian autocracy. . Finland trembles, Sweden trembles, Poland trembles and not to mention Germany, Spain, England, in everything related to energy and food, but also to security and defense, since Vladimir Putin's officials, far from calming the waters , repeat like a mantra the possibility of a Third World War, and at the height of their alarmist propaganda they broadcast spots where they simulate the nuclear catastrophe with which they could destroy Berlin in 106 seconds, Paris in 3 minutes, and London in less than four.

What we are seeing with our eyes is day after day how Putin has faithfully learned from whom he himself called one of his favorite consultants, the German-American war criminal Henry Kissinger, who without any effort to disguise it considers Putin to be a true geopolitical genius, who since 2014 has been announcing much of what happened. Henry Kissinger has, for example, managed to get his traditional bosses, the Rockefellers, to prevent Russia from falling into default in exchange for increasing his decisive stake in the gas industry that Putin has ceded to them.

In the case of Putin, he is our second protagonist today, Bill Gates being the first, having to admit that when I believed that his capacity to do evil could no longer surprise me, at least not as much as it already had, I was completely wrong. There are still deluded people who believe that this war is foreign to them and that its consequences are still far away, completely ignoring the butterfly effect in an increasingly interconnected world. This military and humanitarian catastrophe is accelerating the world's economic and financial impoverishment, a process that results from the irresponsible and unsustainable spending of all politicians, whether they are globalists or nationalists, conservatives or social democrats or pseudo-liberals.

We have been choking on the post-binge vomit for more than a decade, a tax binge of cheap credit, corruption, inflation and statist theft in all its forms. And this failure broke out violently with the 2008 crisis. And then it ended up specifying the institution of a new totalitarianism , of a technocratic, elitist and global socialism, with great fanfare after the Covid pandemic/plandemic , when the bankers and the technological emperors that make up, for example, the Davos Forum or the World Economic Forum, decided to supplant an unsustainable model, that is, that of the old democracies that we knew, for a much worse one that perpetuates and multiplies their concentration of power. More government, less freedom, much more surveillance and goodbye to privacy, more fear and less security and of course more pestilence and less salt, more corporate wealth and much less competent companies, less healthy markets and private property, less energy, less food, more hunger, fewer human beings and more slaves, which is the recipe that literally devised a few centuries ago, the delirious apocalyptic Thomas Malthus, the intellectual father of all this tragedy. But if something was missing, gentlemen, it is the war.

And this war is a new chapter of the great Restart or Reset that is openly announced by Klaus Schwab, president and founder of the World Economic Forum, while at this very moment food prices continue to rise, fertilizer prices have multiplied by five the oil, gas, aluminum, palladium, while the dollar and the euro are aggressively devalued due to circumstantial and deliberate maneuvers by the financial elite. In other words, they are currently devaluing the GDP of all the nations of the world.

In other words, we are being impoverished with unusual speed, and we are the victims of a coordinated attack by all the powerful and their employees. Many of the people who were to plant and harvest the crops of two agricultural mega-powers, Russia, one of the world's largest, and Ukraine, dubbed the breadbasket of Europe, have been forced from their homes, while the black lands Ukrainian women are missing out on crucial planting and harvesting seasons, and sanctions on Russia are wiping out their food and energy production, faster only than the Stalinist Soviet genocide of the 1920s.

In case something was missing to complete the nightmare, the second most powerful Army on the planet, or at least what the big Russian and North American media would have us believe, that is, the Russian Army does not achieve its supposed mission, it is terribly stalled while it seems to speculate rather crudely, that Vladimir Putin suffers from physical and mental disorders, which means that this agonizing war could drag on in time.

Proof of this is a very curious and one could even say suicidal defensive technique that the Ukrainians have implemented, or rather, the Ukrainian politicians to the despair of all their people. We are referring to the fact that they have flooded the black earth plains, a region that is literally the most fertile in the entire globe, causing severe damage that will not only affect this year, but also in the following years, at least until the next five years. , that is, until 2027.

One of the main sources of wheat in the entire world has been artificially injured, all Europeans and half of Asians fill their refrigerators and cupboards with Russian and Ukrainian products. But to make matters worse, the rest of the great food producers on the planet without exception such as the United States , Brazil, Argentina, Mexico, Colombia, to give just a few examples, need fertilizers and pesticides from Russia and Belarus and other chemical products. produced in the Ukraine like the thirsty need water, while the prices of these products, affected by the military battle and the economic battle, have multiplied by five.

Given this, the president of the United States Joe Biden himself is imploring Congress for more budget to alleviate the food crisis, that is, more emissions, more taxes, that is, more cancer to cure AIDS. In this way, shortages are already severely hitting the shelves of the richest country in the world, the United States, and all this gloomy picture benefits an individual, the same man who prophesied the Covid pandemic , that is, Bill Gates, while patenting one of his recipes shortly before, while he consolidated "by chance" as the main financier of the World Health Organization, the same one that patented the confinement policies that generated their companies, with Microsoft at the head, the highest profits in its history, given the artificial increase in demand for Windows and office automation packages for telecommuting and digitalization of small and medium-sized companies, forced to have their employees work from home. He himself financed seven of the fifteen products that the different states that obey him imposed in one way or another on the majority of their citizens.

The truth is that Bill has been painstakingly preparing for years for a famine of biblical proportions, which finds him positioned now that he has just started out as the largest landowner in the United States, that is, as the largest possessor of the best land in North America. By the way, although almost nobody knows it, Bill Gates is also the main tycoon of the food industry of the immediate future. In fact, none of this can be separated from what happened in 2020, it is exactly its continuation, its improved or worsened remake.

The forced closures triggered malnutrition rates throughout the planet, caused hundreds of thousands of competitive companies to go bankrupt due to the political obligation to lower their shutters, generated an optimal breeding ground, that is, a higher number of unemployed than ever had been recorded in universal history, to the point that the director of the United Nations world food program, that is, the same world government project that generated the catastrophe, had already admitted in April 2020 that 820 million people were going to sleep on an empty stomach, and that in the next few months, for the first time in 80 years, 300,000 human beings like you and me would die of hunger every day.

The dream of Malthus or the father of Bill Gates and his friend Margaret Sanger, the geneticists of the 1960s, convinced that the best favor they could do our species was to prune and trim it. In the words of Sanger "annihilate human garbage" and since 2020 what is happening.

At the same time homelessness has increased by 120 percent worldwide and this nightmare has just started very recently. Of course, Gates warned that the worst of the tragedy is yet to be seen, and long-suffering Shanghainese are witnesses that once again the bespectacled philanthropist appears to be right. While again in the spring of 2022 in China, fierce limitations are applied to freedom of movement under the pretext of a new wave of

Covid , this being the cruelest of all the experiments carried out in that nation.

By the way, China or rather, the Chinese Communist Party, positioned as the great winner of the contest between Russia and Ukraine, although ironically today in its most populous city, Shanghai, fifteen million people cry and scream desperately begging for food from their prison home, to which basic products do not arrive and from which they cannot leave because circulation is prohibited. While in the port of Shanghai, which is the main port in the world, 500 ships are crowded waiting to unload merchandise, many of which rot while thousands of containers are stacked uselessly.

The geopolitical consequences are already visible to all, imports are being suspended. Another big problem for Latin America, whose main client is China, far above the United States and Europe, even when added between the war and Covid , the costs of the world food program grew by 71 million dollars a month, and this has not been enough to avoid having to reduce the daily rations of its barely 3.8 million people assisted. In other words, we have 1 billion homeless people largely thanks to the UN. But they only help four million of those 1,000, and even so this is a literal phrase from the director, we will take food from the hungry to give it to the starving, an official who, to no one's surprise, received a scholarship more than a decade ago in the Foundation of our protagonist.

Put in the context of this slow gradual holocaust like the famous torments of ancient China, forgive the redundancy we will proceed to explain how Bill Gates is directly linked to Vladimir Putin's kleptocracy , with Putin himself and with this war crisis that is realizing his evil dream of dominating a humanity that is extinct hour after hour, so let's address the first question, that is, how Bill Gates landed in Russia

The fall of Soviet communism, strictly speaking, was neither expected nor sought by the American elite who for 70 years made the most of its existence. Behind Hitler, Stalin and Roosevelt stood the same unscrupulous Wall Street bankers and American industrialists like Henry Ford, among many others, seduced by the creation of huge captive markets controlled by strong and authoritarian governments, they became monopoly clients of the companies who supported their regimes, eradicating their competition if necessary by shooting. This dynamic by which the Second World War was reached is perfectly documented in the trilogy of the professor at the University of Göttingen, Anthony Sutton

And this dynamic also gave way to Bretton Woods and, if you will, to the Great Restart of the 20th century, continuing later with the Cold War, in which Washington and Moscow divided the globe in two, waging battles on foreign soil, in such a way that they would never they attacked their respective territories and populations, and instead established 1,000 and an agreement of mutual convenience.

But socialism, as Frédéric Bastiat and later Lutwig Von Mises would fall under his own weight, and before the fatal outcome of the Soviet model that began to be glimpsed in the 1980s, the visits of new Western lobbyists began, eager to obtain some benefit from the breakdown of the system.

Gorbachev's famous Perestroika and the first delegation under the pretext of the World Jewish Congress that would assist political prisoners in Russia, arrived integrated by Edgar Bronfman , president of the lobby, together with his assistant, the young Jeffrey Epstein C.

Yes that same pedophile, along with Georgie Warts yes, aka George Soros. But after the fall of the Berlin wall, a second wave of investors arrived willing to share the ashes of the late superpower, the youngest and most peculiar of all was none other than William Bill Gates.

When the cold war was thawing, Microsoft was already there like an icebreaker by 1990. The few Soviet computer users at the time hacked everything. Despite this, Microsoft had achieved its first monopoly contract with the Moscow Soviet before the Soviet Union was formally dissolved, supplying Windows 3.0 to old and inefficient computers in the regime's police stations. The only real competition the tech giant had in that country were pirated copies of its own software.

At the beginning of the economic opening that saved 300 million servants of the Russian red terror from extreme misery, the thirty-something Gates had already started his good business streak there, although with the Soviet dictatorship his main challenge was that 99% of the software sold in the nascent Moscow stores he had no license. His employee, the director of Microsoft in Russia, who by the way had previously been the American consul in St. Petersburg, called Russia the superpower of piracy, lamenting the fall of totalitarianism. In other words, Gates was better off with orthodox communism, which declared that then as now, the main cause of discomfort for him was none other than competition, which is the heart of capitalism and for that and for no other reason they wanted to eliminate the competition.

Gates' first visit to Russia took place in April 1990 in a context of convulsions on the brink of civil war, in which the government of George Bush Sr. had emphatically recommended that American citizens avoid any type of trip to the area. In fact, Bill arrived in his private jet wrapped in a thick, non-ecological fur coat, to impose his authority trying to legitimize his company's monopoly in the eyes of consumers who from one day to the next rediscovered salary, money, savings and a minimum of freedom to choose. So Bill went to take them off. According to a report by George Kennan , who was neither more nor less than the American ambassador to Russia, later to stand out as a historian of the diplomacy of both countries, he comments that Bill gave an interview to the regime's television through which he tried to explain the patent system that he intended to establish in Russia, a country that was disintegrating.

When at that precise moment, Gates, absorbed in his verbiage, completely disregarded the fears and even the illusions of the audience regarding the economic opening process. In fact, Bill used a threatening tone that annoyed the channel's authorities, to the point that they interrupted the recording and they invited him to retire. It was then that he received the advice of a much more mature and experienced lobbyist than Gates, Klaus Schwab, who in 1990 had been installed in a hotel for three months preparing his own deals with the desperate outgoing bureaucracy.

In the film "The Lord of War", Nicolas Cage plays the life of the Ukrainian arms dealer Yuri Orlov, who massively bought military equipment.

Klaus Schwab comforted Gates while also and at the same time managed to lower his pride, and together they founded Dialogue, an organization aimed at connecting California's computer industry with Russia under the active sponsorship of the World Economic Forum. In 1993, Microsoft's representative offices moved from the modest apartment it occupied to a modern building entirely built for the company's headquarters.

And so the first Microsoft subsidiary arose in Moscow, whose main mission was to enforce its abusive corporate licenses, hiring an army of lawyers and bribing key officials from end to end of the immense Eurasian nation, among the latter, the then director of business of the mayor of St. Petersburg, whose real power far exceeded that of Mayor Anatoli Sobchak , that is, Vladimir Vladimirovich Putin. In this way, Putin became a true czar of the national economy from his small position in St. Petersburg, through which he absorbed control of Russia's main port in the midst of chaos, managing operations as diverse as the installation of factories of Coca-Cola, the trafficking of women, permits for private schools, everything, absolutely everything passed through Putin's office or his subordinates. Putin personally pushed Bill Gates' restrictive policies, and in 1995 he was one of the executive consultants to the operational investigations law that gave the Russian secret service, the FSB, the authority to monitor by court order all private communications, from the postal correspondence to cell phone calls and email messages, and all this with a single provider that was Microsoft, an octopus that extended its tentacles to all corners of Boris Yeltsin's alcoholic administration.

After his betrayal of Anatoli Sobchak , Putin was precisely awarded the command of the FSB. This intelligence force that reinvented the KGB, that espionage agency to which Putin himself belonged, which taught him in his youth to spy, manipulate, extort and poison anyone who got in his way.

It was that same year with Olga Dergunova , director of Microsoft in Russia, that Gates' company began giving anti-piracy courses to Putin's agents. In a 2004 interview with Olga Dergunova , she made it clear that in the 1990s the Russians could not even imagine the concept of intellectual property and that it was urgent to persuade them with the force of the law. But Olga Dergunova proudly added that thanks to her management, "now all of Russia knows how Microsoft's patents should be protected and how much to pay Bill Gates." Dergunova focused her persecution against the big vendors of duplicate software, subjected them to million-dollar lawsuits, extortion, and Putin himself voluntarily participated in the hearings, intimidating the judges and receiving in return a generous donation for his own political armoury. By the time Gates returned to Moscow in '97, piracy had dropped by a modest 12%. The first thing Gates did was meet with Boris Yelsin 's number two , Deputy Prime Minister Anatoli Chubáis , who shortly after and until March of this year 2022, would end up serving as Putin's official liaison with transnational organizations , which he has just escape from Russia recently.

After seeing Chubais for the first time, Gates visited the Central Bank Governor, Sergei Dubinin , and closing a US$65 million annual deal gave him access to the information of the country's largest bank, Sberank . This contract that has been revalidated 27 times and is still in force despite the alleged cessation of sales to private parties declared by Microsoft to the press on March 4, 2022. In Moscow there is not a single office that has really closed its doors in the country, and if there is someone in Russia, you can already tell us if this is so or not.

Gates, obsessed with expanding his empire, personally met with Putin and insisted that the problem of piracy was very serious and that its solution could not be postponed. Gates and Putin officially met face to face, and two years later Putin advanced to his last step before taking absolute power, his tenure as Boris Yeltsin's prime minister. At the time, Putin himself bragged to television cameras that he had arrested 76 hackers who were selling cracked Windows. Two weeks later Novaya Gazeta , which was a newspaper that could still be considered pro-government, warned with concern that four of those adolescent prisoners had suffered torture and one of them, Serguei PodKing , just 17 years old, had died of suffocation, all for "stealing" some pennies from Bill Gates, and "steal him" is in quotes because there is an interesting debate in liberalism about intellectual property and patents, since the abuse of patents is the antithesis of private property.

At this time the humanitarian emperor of operating systems, Bill, was laughing happily with his close friend, President Clinton, designing together the new order of the free world. In this way, the relationship between Vladimir Putin, already president of Russia for the first time, and Republican president George Bush, was frankly unbeatable, that is, they were close friends, Putin being the first person to call Bush after the September 11 attacks of 2001 and being the second Bill Gates. Both the Russian and Gates actively collaborated with the genocidal invasion of Afghanistan, the first Putin lending Russian soil for US troops to transit on their way to the massacre of civilians that would extend for the next two decades, the only case in the 1,000 years of Russian history.

Putin thus allowed the Americans to pass through his country to invade another which , by the way, that other country, Afghanistan, had been the reason for the end of the fall of the Soviet Union.

In fact, the second to benefit from the war in Afghanistan was Gates, with his first evaluation of military glasses that are now augmented reality glasses, one of the many products where Microsoft profits from the industry of death and that began precisely at the dawn of the 21st century a little later, specifically on June 20, 2003. Subsequently, the relationship between Bill Gates and the Kremlin took a major leap for the first time, as Microsoft gave the Russian government access to its secret source code, that is, the Russian government was able to access the source code of Windows systems to improve security and strictly annihilate user security.

This is quite curious because until now not even the United States federal government and its security agencies had access to this source code. In fact, the former director of Microsoft in Russia, Olga Dergunova , explained that the company gave up the architecture behind Windows to prevent Putin from switching to a cheaper alternative, inaugurating with Russia a government security program, not to mention mega espionage, that Microsoft would continue with China in 2005 and with its host nation, the United States.

In 2008 to make this situation even worse, part of this agreement included a confidential section of Microsoft with the Federal Agency for Communications and Government Information, a former branch of the KGB, an equivalent to the National Security Agency of the United States, which later I would denounce Edward Snowden. In this way Novaya Gazeta denounced that the secret deal between Putin and Gates included spying on journalists critical of the regime through Windows, which would effectively end up becoming a key tool to locate and assassinate one of the bravest chroniclers of the Novaya Gazeta , Anna

Politkovskaya, opponent executed in front of her young children, in an interview given to the Financial Times by her friends the Rothschilds.

The tyrant Putin claimed that Bill Gates had given the world a taste of his superior intelligence by trusting Russia, and months after this report, on November 7, 2006, the Microsoft Business Forum conference took place in Moscow. On that evening for the first time the new tsar and the then richest man in the world shook hands in public, reaping warm applause from the audience. Then, with the taxes of the suffering Russian taxpayers, Gates was paid a whopping four million dollars to participate in a personal capacity for four hours in the information technology and innovation forum, which was organized by Dimitri Medvedev , Putin's chief of staff. and a future puppet president, assisted by Leonid Reiman, the Russian technology minister. Medvédev and Reiman were also prominent members of the program of young leaders of the world economic forum, that is, other subjects of Klaus Schwab, in line with the negotiations that were already taking place in Spain at the hands of the socialist Rodríguez Zapatero, and in the province of Buenos Aires with the Peronist Daniel Scioli.

Bill Gates agreed to the Internet connection of all schools in Russia and, like Soros, achieved the reform of the Soviet educational system with the support of Sobchak , Chubáis and Putin. In 1994, Gates undertook to oversee Medvedev and Reiman 's computer education project . As a result of the new contract, the International Technological University was born, the Russian High-Tech School, where all the high-ranking officers in charge of brutally repressing and even making demonstrators disappear in the recent protests in Kazakhstan were educated.

Reiman, the Putin minister closest to Gates and Schwab, was the same subject who on July 25, 2000, a few months before Putin took office, issued the 130th order allowing the Kremlin to spy on internet transmissions. of its citizens without the need for a court order, that is, at the will of the president, that is, a pioneering experiment that was incredibly one year ahead of the Patriot Act of George Bush son himself, and for many years it was ahead of the Prisma project continued by Obama, in which Microsoft would also play a leading role. From then on, the possibility of maintaining a truly private browsing, or a secure correspondence within Windows, at least in any of the 11 regions of the Russian Federation, disappeared forever. It is curious that this same law has made it easier today, in the context of the war in Russia and Ukraine, for the Putin government to block Instagram and Twitter but never block Microsoft. According to political analyst Boris Viceski , Mr. Reiman is one of Putin's closest intimates, and one of the officials who during his time in St. Petersburg served as a link between him and the mafia, a man who carries the virus of corruption. in the depths of his veins.

At the end of 2011, the Frankfurt Public Prosecutor's Office would accuse Reiman and his lawyer Jeffrey Gall of participating in a scheme to launder money from human trafficking in the 1990s, which involved the Commerzbank of Germany. Gates's other favorite interlocutor was Medvedev , considered a " tech " guy , or knowledgeable and savvy about technology. Medvedev is a fan of cutting-edge technology who, when he symbolically replaced Putin in 2010, would end up embarking on a personal tour of Silicon Valley seeking advice on setting up a similar tech hub dubbed Inno Groove outside Moscow. Meanwhile, Putin wielded real power as prime minister again

Medvedev 's reception in San Francisco was led by the Governor of California, Arnold Schwarzenegger himself, the most progressive of all Republicans. Later he visited Gates, stopped by Apple and Twitter, and even had meetings with executives from Cisco and Google. This visit had the objective of maintaining the strong friendship between Putin's Russia and the United States that began the Obama era. The proposal was called Russia Reset , yes the reset of Russia, and we emphasize again that both Putin and Medvedev They are close friends of the one who now sells us the

Great World Reset or Great Reset , that is, of Klaus Schwab. By the way, the master of ceremonies in charge of opening the event was Secretary of State Hillary Clinton, who was later accompanied by her smiling financier of the Clinton Global Initiative for the imposition of feminism and abortion and birth control policies, a certain Melinda Gates, then Bill's wife. Both sponsored and presented the event of the big hug between Russia and the United States, that is, the Reset of the old rivals. In this way Hillary brandished a red plastic button that said " Reset " presented by Sergei Lavrov , the same chancellor who today in 2022 is in charge of threatening us all with the nuclear annihilation of life on Earth. Part of the Russian reset was the creation of Skolkovo , an industrial enclave near Moscow, in the image and likeness of the tech stock in Mountain View, California. The idea was to encourage American companies to help with both technology and expansion in exchange for privileges that would limit their competitors and kidnap Russian buyers. In this context, the secret connections between Hillary Clinton, the Clinton Foundation and Victor Vekselberg , a mysterious Russian tycoon who is a personal friend and protégé of Putin, director of finances for a time of the united Russia, that is, the treasurer , began to be revealed. of the party and owner of Renova Group , a corporation with tentacles in the aluminum, oil, energy and telecommunications sectors, all four sectors being directly regulated by Putin.

Vekselberg was in charge of coordinating the future Skolkovo project , but the star company of these investments was none other than Microsoft. Gates's appointed CIO or chief information officer, Steve Ballmer, signed a lengthy memorandum of understanding with Vekselberg , the futuristic oligarch. A study published by the Government accountability Institute detailed that some 30,000 workers selected by the Gates team worked in this Russian geek pole (which is passionate about technology) under strict government control.

The magnitude of the contract with Microsoft in 2010 was such that Microsoft returned to deliver its new private codes, this time to the Armed and Security Forces as a whole, helped Russia to develop cryptography and computer weapons of the highest quality, which are the same that currently the hypocritical Western media and the White House itself point to as triggering a global information war, which could lead to the third panic event planned by the Davos Forum , the Cyber Polygon or great internet blackout, whose drill similar to event 201 that heralded the global outbreak of Covid was carried out in Russia, since in 2020 and 2021 the Western elite with Putin in Russia made two simulations of computer warfare . Do you realize to what extent we are following a real script written by all the actors pretending to rival each other?

In its day, the FBI issued a high alert to Hillary Clinton's State Department, stating that through this contract they were handing military technology to a foreign power on a silver platter, but Hillary deliberately decided to put the warnings in the drawer and give He gave Gates free rein to continue with his program, while Ukraine's president , Zelensky , another exemplary student of Klaus Schwab, protests that the Russians are hacking Ukraine, whether they are hacking the government or its citizens.

Zelensky should also direct his criticism at the visionary Bill Gates, who disguises himself as the savior of the world, and at the couple who have dominated the destinies of the United States, the Clintons, for 30 years. As the latest proof of the crime of high treason committed by both Hillary and Bill Gates, only two months after the alliance sealed by Medvedev and Obama, it became clear that the police warnings were not unfounded fears. The FBI revealed the existence of 11 Russian sleeper spies who had been living covertly in the United States since the early 2000s, who were illegals who, after perfect training and falsification of identities, posed as American citizens from the suburbs. who worked and raised their children near Boston, New York and Washington.

Putin 's intelligence , reminded these agents via an encrypted message to seek out and develop ties in political circles, and to send information immediately. Ten of the accused pleaded guilty in July and the 11th had fled to Cyprus and apparently escaped back to Moscow. While the other spies did not stay in the United States or go to Guantánamo prison, and did not suffer the fate that they want the heroic Julian Assange to die in prison, but were returned to Russia. Literally unbelievable as it may seem, they were returned to Putin, as Obama took the spies and traded them at the Vienna airport for four traitors convicted of working as a CIA informant behind the Iron Curtain.

Finally Putin met with the deported spies, and sang and celebrated with them loudly. But what does Bill Gates have to do with all this? Four of the eleven detected spies worked in software stores, but 3 weeks later the 12th spy, Alexei Karetnikov, appeared, an unusual young Russian agent who worked for Microsoft, according to the details published by the FBI that you can verify yourself. Karetnikov settled in Redmond, a city in the State of Washington, where Microsoft has its world headquarters, working for 9 months as an employee of Putin and from there at the same time testing products and maintaining communications with his 11 colleagues at just 20 years of age, Karetnikov was subsequently arrested for violations of immigration law, and was immediately deported, inexplicably saving him from the judicial process that corresponded to him. Just after boarding the plane, an FBI official updated his profile stating that Karetnikov operated for Neobit, a small Romanian corporation whose only client was the Russian Ministry of Defense. No Microsoft executives were called to testify.

Due to the strange illegal hiring of this boy, the detective who investigated the case was prematurely retired at the age of 43

As far as internal repression is concerned, the alliance with Microsoft became increasingly powerful, despite Bill Gates's repeated environmental discourse ad nauseam since the early 1990s. In September 2010, Russian plainclothes policemen came to Baikal Environment headquarters Way , an environmental NGO that denounced Putin's polluting policies, and without saying a word they immobilized the security guard, ripped the cables from their computers and took them away. Terrified activists had to abort their thought-secret plan to stage a protest against the opening of a paper mill, which they say was poisoning Russia's Lake Baikal, which contains no less than 20% of the world's fresh water. . The authorities' excuse for taking the computers was simply to confiscate their pirated copies of Windows.

This whole show of breaking into the office, taking the computers, knocking out the security guard, was to confiscate the pirated copies of Windows. Over the past decade, Microsoft's lawsuits in Russia have become the most numerous on the planet, serving as an excuse for the Kremlin to wage dozens of raids and raids against dissidents, journalists and even tourists.

When police seized computers from two critical newspapers in the city of Samara, editor Sergei Kurtadisev said that without Microsoft's involvement, these criminal cases against journalists would not exist. The Putin Government uses Windows to cover up the extermination of civil rights. In this way, human rights organizations in the United States and the Cato Institute , which is a think tank libertarian tank , asked Bill Gates' firm for explanations for this abominable practice. The response they received was none other than Microsoft's lawyers in Russia, firmly backing Putin in his fight against piracy and confirming that they, the quasi-monopolists of operating systems on the globe, were in fact the real victims. of this whole thing.

The fact is that this criminal pact between the king of Silicon Valley and the Kremlin chief was gaining too much public notoriety. To dissipate the strong controversy in the coming years, all the contracts were maintained, but without the obscene displays of affection of the past. After the invasion of Crimea in 2014 and the 180º turn of the Western discourse towards Russia in 2016, the Kremlin launched an overactive campaign that swore to get rid of any foreign corporation that is dangerous to its interests. Some government offices were purged of some foreign software, beginning with the replacement of Windows with Russian products. However, not only did Microsoft not cease its operations, much less reduce suggestions in Russia, but it also took advantage of this new circumstance. Another suspiciously timed fluke for Bill Gates. In January 2016, Roskomnadzor, Putin 's telecommunications regulator , began a legal battle to block the professional network LinkedIn, assuming that it did not respect the privacy of its users. Russia, complaining about the privacy of Russians. What a good joke! Given that the Russian market was very important for the platform, among other things because of the constant unemployment and stagnation suffered by that nation for many years, the news gained great visibility and during the first week of February the shares of this company plummeted a 43%, with Putin's maneuver being one of its main reasons.

And guess who jumped at the chance to get LinkedIn at a bargain price? Exactly, Microsoft, overcoming resistance, the corporation founded and still directed by Bill Gates took over LinkedIn for the sum of 26,000 million dollars, half of its price estimated by JP Morgan in its best moments. During the government of Donald Trump, who despite the alleged roughness maintained with Gates, drastically multiplied military purchases from Microsoft. At that time another incredibly revealing fact came to light, in 2019 the investigative portal Open Media took on the task of examining some of the official photographs published by the press office of the Russian Presidency, and they realized that Vladimir Putin still had installed Windows XP on their personal computers in 2019. In this way, the leader of the supposed rival hyperpower of the United States, continued to use the most emblematic product of the American computer industry, both in his computer in the Kremlin office and in his official residence in Novo Organovo , near Moscow.

You don't have to be a genius to realize what it means that the owner of the largest nuclear arsenal on the planet, the president of

Russia, directly entrusts his communications, his documents, his private information to Bill Gates.

The globalist elite and the Russian state were and are perfect synonyms. Naturally , in 2020, Microsoft gave its friend Putin free equipment to combat Covid , while the mutual friend, Klaus Schwab, made juicy deals with Putin's Sputnik vaccine , and as usual, they declared their love for each other in public. "Dear friend, I have had the pleasure of visiting you for 30 years," Putin told Schwab, "fulfilling his role as the opening of the Davos Forum cyberconference , to later become the host of the computer pandemic drill or the great blackout, also known as Cyber Polygon , literally an event that heralds an information war and where big Western corporations willingly handed over data to their supposed spectral enemy, which is the Russian government. Once again, Microsoft managed Putin's health policies plus Putin himself did, providing cloud services for remote work of white staff, sharing access directly with the government, and Microsoft performing official statistical analyzes for hospital facilities.

Putin and Gates would once team up at Covax , the Global Access Fund for Covid-19 Vaccines .

Concluding this first stage after an arduous investigation, we have shown sufficient evidence that Vladimir Putin is one of the essential partners of Bill Gates at the height of Chi Jinping, and of submissive presidents like López Obrador, like Trudeau, like Macron, Lula da Silva , Pedro Sánchez or all the North American presidents, with the exception of the one who stepped to the other side of the counter, the eternal Bill Clinton.

Next we will continue with the second part of this book answering the question about how Bill Gates carefully positioned himself to strengthen himself from this war. In fact , in the first instance, the answer is obvious, the information war, as stated in the statement of April 7, 2022, signed by Tom Berge , corporate vice president of security at Microsoft, since Gates' firm has taken sides in the cyber military conflict in the supposed defense of Ukraine, neutralizing potential Russian attacks carried out in part with the technology provided years earlier by Microsoft to Russia. As the saying goes, you have to put eggs in all baskets, and it goes without saying that the expenses of this "operation shield" are borne by the squeezed taxpayers of the United States, as this server is part of the economic aid package of the Biden administration to the Zelensky government . All this is an absolute minutiae compared to the fact that since the beginning of Russia's military invasion of Ukraine, the North American complex, that is, the military and arms sector of heavy industry, has multiplied its activity by 8, and Microsoft got a juicy contract in May 2022, for 22,000 million dollars from the Biden Government to provide HoloLens helmets, which include the famous augmented reality glasses to both US soldiers and Ukrainian soldiers, in the best style of the Rothschild Bill Gates is present on both sides. In fact, this contract brought the historical record of gains in military sales, in the very long history of the commercial relationship between Microsoft and the United States Department of Defense.

However, since the scandal caused by his involvement in the 2020 crisis, added to his close friendship with the late child trafficker Jeffrey Epstein, Bill Gates has taken a symbolic distance from Microsoft, being removed from the board. Despite keeping one of his main packages of shares, no matter how much impunity his money can buy, Gates has become, according to the Sundance pollster , the most repudiated public figure in recent years.

He himself has complained at the end of May 2022 in an interview with the Today cycle , of the British state network BBC, that he cannot go out in the street in peace because people insult him frantically.

Not so long ago that Microsoft's leadership announced that its honorary president, Bill Gates, chose to close his 40-year tenure as director to devote himself fully to philanthropy, while today hardly anyone is unaware at this point that the Foundation Bill and Melinda Gates is the most influential NGO on the planet.

Nobody is surprised that many of the laboratories that the Bill and Melinda Gates Foundation sponsors and finances are profiting from the hundreds of thousands of wounded, civilians and military, that this Russian war against Ukraine throws.

However, the third reason for economic joy for Bill Gates, taking advantage of the artificially created tragedy of the energy and food crisis, and we will show how Bill Gates built step by step a gigantic food empire thanks to privileged information, among other providers, provided by Putin and with crucial partners linking him to both the Russian and Ukrainian oligarchy, and to Volodymir Zelenskyy's inner circle. Gates' tentacles reach far beyond GM seeds, also hypermarkets, one of which will surely be familiar to you, plus food-carrying railroads and some of the best-known hamburger chains and food brands. .

We are certainly eating Bill Gates products and many have no idea what Gates plans to do with his food.

BILL GATES AND HOW HE BECAME A TYCOON IN THE AGRICULTURAL AND FOOD SECTOR. ITS INFLUENCE ON THE CURRENT FOOD CRISIS.

In the previous chapters, we unfolded a perfect map of the investment histories of Microsoft and its founder Bill Gates in

Russia from 1990 to the present. We also discovered on the part of Gates and Microsoft a highly oiled commercial and political relationship with the government of Vladimir Putin, who offered great favors to the brand by rigorously tackling computer hacking, even before he was president of Russia. But since Putin became the tenant of the Kremlin, the new czar of Russia, he obtained incredible things from Microsoft, such as access to its source code years before the United States government itself obtained it, and thus facilitating the surveillance of all Russian computers under the pretext of defending Bill Gates' corporate patents, managing to raid offices and confiscate devices of prominent journalists and political opponents.

Russian spies in the United States working directly at Microsoft headquarters in Redmond, Washington state. Lawyers for the firm praising Putin's actions when this controversy was brought to their attention, and even deals that categorically involved Russian oligarchs from Putin's circle alongside leading members of the Western political class, reaching the peak of this collaboration entirely unknown in our countries with the so-called Russian Reset , which had its inaugural act with a reset button, a handshake and everything between Foreign Minister Lavrov and Barack Obama's then Secretary of State, Hillary Clinton. All of this has led to new billion-dollar contracts for Gates and a degree of trust with the Russian leader, reaching the point that Putin, who is considered by many to be the statesman most hostile to the Western world, trusts nothing more or less than his own personal computers to the bespectacled philanthropist. In short, a connection worthy of but as real as the economic crisis that is plaguing the world.

Next we will tell you another chapter of this story, which is precisely the global food energy disaster that has generated the Russian invasion of Ukraine, and that answers why our protagonist, Bill Gates, without a doubt, all "a farsighted" was preparing for years for this scenario, conquering a decisive influence in each and every one of the strategic sectors in the production and distribution of food, which is already a fundamental good for our lives, which, as we will see below, is not guaranteed to anyone.

Gates has made a radical and masterful turn to his heritage, going from high technology to the primary link in the economy and like it or not we have much to learn about it.

In fact , the war came with a terrible situation regarding the supply of conventional energy or fossil energy, oil and gas to the world market, which is already causing many European citizens, starting with the Poles, to be cold in their own homes, a dystopian reality very close to German society where there is real social panic in the face of the bankruptcy of its industry, the most thriving on the continent, which is extremely dependent on Russian gas. For its part, the Russian economy is very poor in relation to its number of inhabitants and wealth is extremely concentrated in the hands of Putin and his friends the oligarchs, but we cannot neglect that being the largest nation on planet Earth, it is rich and very influential when it comes to "commodities " of raw materials, depending exclusively on the export of oil. Russia is the world's third-largest exporter of crude after the United States, thanks to fracking , and Saudi Arabia, and is the number one exporter of natural gas before the self-styled special military operation. Russia provided one of every 10 barrels of oil consumed globally, that is, 40% of the fuel in the European Union and 25% of the gas that passes through Ukraine, through the invaded territory that, by the way, includes strategic gas pipelines . Today, the missiles that take innocent lives in Kiev or Mariupol are bought with the gasoline of European cars. A great paradox is that the sanctions that hundreds of countries are applying against Russia have caused the oil market to face its greatest turbulence since the 1970s and the OPEC crisis.

There is no capacity that can replace the Russian production of 5 million barrels of oil per day, and regarding the price of gas, we must say that despite all attempts to contain inflation, it has shot up 30% in the last 12 weeks. Brazil and Great Britain registered record rates in the last days of May and first days of June 2022, and in China the government asked the oil companies to suspend exports of gasoline and diesel. In Spain, kilometric queues of people have been seen waiting at service stations at gas stations, from 12:00 at night until the next morning, everything is to fill the tank. Prices in the United States, where gas also fulfills the specific function of drying grains, the grains that both people and livestock eat have exceeded the maximum limits of the 2008 crisis. In fact, several border cities testify how day after Every day Americans cross into Mexico to load Gasoline in states like Chihuahua, many of them are the same ones that demanded that Clinton, Obama and Trump raise and enlarge the border wall, and even ruthlessly shoot at immigrants who dare to cross it.

Energy and food are connected at various levels, so for example the very fertilizers that half of humanity needs to live are made from oil, and for example think for a moment about the plastic containers in which an immense amount and variety of what today routinely every week, every month, every year, throughout our lives we put in our mouths.

And now, Russia and Ukraine are crucial exporters like 25-30% of total wheat exports, also almost 20% of corn exports. Ukraine is the main supplier of corn and the world's largest manufacturer of sunflower oil. Russia ranks second in this ranking and between the two nations they take 60 percent of global production. In fact the Russians don't sell more because of the sanctions, while the Ukrainians can't because they are cut off by Russian forces blockading their main seaports, while 30% of the farmland is in war, and the rest of the land has not been occupied because it was recklessly and suicidally flooded by the Zelensky government to prevent an occupation of those lands, which is a very strange way of defending the territory, flooding it until it is disable their most precious sources of food production, but time after time they will understand what is hidden behind this curious defensive tactic.

As usual, it is the poorest countries in the world that are beginning to suffer: Lebanon. Yemen, Syria and Tunisia consume 50% of food produced in Ukraine. Saudi Arabia, in turn a partner of both the United States and Russia, celebrates a new punishment against the long-suffering Yemenis, whom they are annihilating by the tens of thousands in a fierce war that no one talks about despite the fact that it has been underway for already several years.

Now with the war, the German supplies are similar to the Venezuelan ones. There are not only ration quotas for oil but also for flour. In Sweden, restrictions are applied to family consumption of powdered milk, pasta, cereals, canned foods, whose prices have skyrocketed by 20%, and baked goods. In Spain completely empty shelves abound.

Regarding the omnipresent fertilizers in the production of all kinds of vegetables, not only does the affected region produce 25% of these products internationally, but specifically between both sides, Russia and Ukraine take 42% of total sales of urea, the specific variant of fertilizers that drastically improves the yield of potato, rice, corn, sugar cane and all vegetables. Only 4,000 million people, that is, half of humanity, could survive if the flow of urea is totally cut off. Take accounts. In fact, food-producing countries such as the United States, Brazil, Argentina or Colombia are already seriously suffering their markets instead of benefiting from these sanctions, precisely because the prices of fertilizers multiplied by five.

Some wonder why the president of Brazil, Bolsonaro, supports Putin? It is not only because of Putin's feigned traditionalist discourse, which, as our investigations have already made clear, is much more Stalinist than nostalgic for the czars. The reality is that Brazil, the main soybean producer on the planet, could lose more than half of its harvest without Russian fertilizers, and currently it only has 3 months of reserves left and that soybean, that is, the Brazilian, the Argentine, the Paraguayan is the one that China buys to feed its cattle, which represents the absolute majority of the proteins of those more than 1,300 million individuals that account for a sixth of the world population. OR

A particularly sick and worrying situation about the war in Ukraine is the issue of dehydration of people who are holed up in basements, fending off Russian bombs. And it is that the aforementioned strategy of planned floods is not only suicidal because it floods the fields near the capital, but also makes the roads of the Ukrainian towns impassable, makes it difficult for citizens to escape and obstructs the evacuation of civilians. It is suicidal, moreover, because it is generating the worst of all problems, which is the shortage of drinking water, something that is not new to Ukraine, but which has been aggravated by this tactic.

Much of the pipes are irreversibly damaged and repairs are completely stopped. If we go by the World Health Organization, of which Bill Gates is its main private financier, and the second in general terms after China, by 2025 the problem will not only be Ukraine, but half of the inhabitants of the planet are located in areas with scarcity of drinking water.

Hence Gates' historic investment to convert sewage, sewage, water with fecal waste into supposedly suitable water for human consumption, a project that he has popularized in the Netflix promotional series about himself, and which has earned him the multiplication of memes. Would you drink a glass of purified water from Bill Gates?

We see how from his ecological mansion of 97 million dollars, Gates contemplates how the world burns, just as Emperor Nero contemplated how Rome burned, but of course, Nero burned Rome and Bill Gates burned the world placidly.

On the shores of Lake Washington, in the paradisiacal forests that approach the city, the eco-digital mansion connected to a database has a tiny chip that the technocrat places on the collar of his shirt and as he goes through his house , your favorite music plays and the television screens are filled with images that calm your spirits: images like the price of oil, stations full of cars, empty supermarket shelves, and refugees dying of hunger and thirst. In his 2019 book, Gates had already realized that his beloved advisory board, including the Russians, had motivated him to liquidate all his holdings in oil and gas companies, as he actually recounted in an interview with the magazine British The Economist.

In February 2019, he said that he was selling the few shares he had left in companies indirectly related to fossil fuels, and when asked why, he simply replied that he was preparing for the next catastrophe.

In fact, the former Secretary of State and current director of the Council On Foreign Relations and the Bilderberg Club, protégé and associate of the Rockefellers, Henry Kissinger, a certain author of the NSSM-200 plan for population reduction in Latin America, once said that whoever controls the food supply controls the people. Back in the 90s of the 20th century, the Bill and Melinda Gates Foundation established their public health and education programs, but starting in 2006, Bill and Melinda took the advice of their friend Kissinger very seriously, let us not forget that he is also Putin's advisor, and from that moment they consolidated a true food empire thanks to the impulse of a first donation from the financial speculator Warren Buffett, who in other times knew how to be the best friend of Bill Gates.

At the time, Buffet was in a hurry to write off some of the massive tax debt he had acquired during the Bush administration. The Gates began with a powerful agricultural development program that sought a strategic ally with an immense track record in the food sector, the Rockefeller Foundation. The Rockefeller model was the self-confessed inspiration of George Soros, for example, for the opening of his Soros Foundation, later known as the Open Society . Foundations , being the Rockefeller Foundation, a paradigm in the philanthropy industry, and the same entity that once financed the research of the agronomist Norman Borlaug , father of the so-called green revolution. Borlaug , received a well-deserved Nobel Peace Prize because his scientific research work in the area of transgenics led to the genetic improvement of wheat, corn and many other crops that became more resistant and productive from then on, which It allowed maximizing the yield of lands that were not so advantageous. Borlaug is considered the man who more lives, except in the history of mankind, prevented 700 million Asians from dying of hunger imminently.

However, how could it be otherwise, the Rockefellers had no humanitarian intention and obtained what they were initially looking for, the monopoly patents of the most innovative agro-technology of the 70s. The fact is that half a century later , the Gates couple and the next generation of the Rockefeller dynasty created the alliance for a green revolution in Africa, called AGRA, an initial project of 424 million dollars with which they promised to double the productivity of crops, empower farmers and improve drastically your quality of life.

However, unlike Borlaug , who turned to the desperate pleas for help from Indians and Pakistanis in his investigations, in this case the African peasants had never asked the Gateses or anyone else for help.

Although perhaps unknown to a certain extent, the problem of hunger in Africa is exclusively political and corrupt politicians, including brutal dictators Bill and Melinda armed themselves when it came to reconquering the African continent. Perhaps nothing similar to the European industrial revolution has appeared in Africa, but tribal agricultural practices developed a process analogous to the current genetic improvement of crops via the laboratory. What do we mean? That the Africans took a millennium of tradition to achieve identical or even better results, promoting the diversity of crops, studying seasonality, that is, when it is best to plant each crop, fine-tuning a strict selection of the best seeds and mixing them with each other to achieve certain results, and in turn promoting the decentralization of land through inheritance, framed in a market system that fostered competition long before the Europeans came to impose their imperial yoke in the nineteenth century.

Although it is true that before European imperialism there were predatory and oppressive hegemonies, for example, the Zulus in South Africa, who were similarly brutal to the Incas in South America, in African culture, personal freedom occupies a very important factor. . And a long time ago, specifically I am referring to the sub-Saharan clans, where each of the families made their own decisions with great autonomy and within families individuals could peacefully separate and join other tribes, as we said, both inheritance and agrarian private property were institutions fully rooted in the most fertile valleys, which translated into continuous innovation by millions of small and medium-sized farmers interested in improving their products.

Anyone who has visited, even in recent years, the quietest African countries, that is, those that have not been particularly convulsed by dictatorship, by civil wars or by foreign operations, for example Botswana, Ghana or Sierra Leone, anyone Anyone who has visited knows well that even the humblest families regularly enjoy great banquets. And it is that in Africa there are shortages of all kinds, but food, at least in the sub-Saharan territories where there is peace, was never a problem.

Logically, Bill Gates's colonialist crusade does not aim to solve problems that do not exist, but precisely to create them, obeying the old statist premise of breaking legs to deliver crutches, Gates went so far as to dismantle through paramilitary groups the pockets of resistance to its initiatives, and implemented high technology totally centralized by the bureaucrats of its Foundation, articulating monocultures, that is, the same crop permanently on the land, which depletes it and makes it in turn dependent on poorly tested chemicals, even violently appropriating the sources of drinking water in each region where it intervened.

Gates forced small African farms to adopt Rockefeller patented commercial seeds and Russian fertilizers, yes Russian fertilizers.

Continuing with AGRA, the alliance between the Rockefellers and Gates in Africa, so that it is clear who is who in this story, I tell you that starting in 2008 and despite the growing rejection of African citizens, four foreign states began to inject stolen money to its own citizens, of course, which are Belgium, France and Germany. These three ancient powers that carried out the most abominable crimes against humanity in this region of the world, apparently felt some nostalgia for those old days and wanted to repeat the experience, but the fourth, gentlemen, was neither more nor less than Russia , which in its Soviet stage also took advantage of Africa.

In the 20th century, half of Africa was left in the hands of the Europeans and the Americans, and the other half under the clutches of the brutal communists. And it is that Putin is clearly a man who likes to continue with the traditions, not the traditions of Dostoevsky, Tolstoy, Turgenev , and also with the Bolshevik, Leninist, Stalinist, genocidal traditions.

So there was Vladimir Putin giving rubles to Bill Gates's food project in Africa, a close friend of Putin's dictator and also of China, the Zimbabwean Robert Mugabe, helped Gates meet the goal of 23 million farmers affiliated with his program And he did it the only way Mugabe knew how, at gunpoint. An octogenarian Mugabe, who proclaimed himself the Liberator of Zimbabwe, was known worldwide for the massacres in Matabeleland in the 1980s, the massive expropriation of farms, both white and black dissidents, and the fierce repression of the militants of the Democratic Change movement, which included hacking open the living with machetes, removing their intestines, strangling them with them, and hanging them from poles.

Look what people Bill Gates does business with. The Rosa Luxemburg Foundation , belonging to the German communist left and entirely supported by the state, the same state that contributes to the Gates project, participated as an observer of the program in Zimbabwe, highlighting that the collective crops that Mugabe gave to the Gates Foundation They were already unproductive, before the arrival of the North American couple, but with the arrival of Gates's technocrats they directly disappeared if they disappeared. Zimbabwe found itself from one day to the next with no food left and this was one of the causes that, worsening year after year, determined the fall of Mugabe. The real problem, disturbing as it may be, is that not only did the harvest disappear, which the Luxenburg Foundation elliptically attributes to a technical flaw, or to an ambitious design by the Gates Foundation. The truth is that, according to the Zimbabwean press, those who disappeared were more than 2,000 people like you and me, who after a strike against their strict training in these new techniques that they completely rejected, were never seen again.

It is incredible that both Mugabe and Gates received the Confucius prize for peace, the equivalent of the Chinese Communist Party's Nobel Prize, while their friends in Beijing kept one after another with the great infrastructure works in Africa, Bill chose to associate himself with Shi Jinping to carry out the gigantic ghost train that connects Kenya, Uganda, the Democratic Congo and Rwanda, being the main grain transport route in Africa. Coincidentally, the Gates Foundation led to the landing of other of its official partners, its partners of the World Wide Fund , the world's leading environmental fund, best known, for example, for being the number one donor to Greenpeace, while Gates progressively took over agricultural production. African, the double World Wife Fund was in charge of implementing its most convincing animal policies, its strictest measures against the consumption of meat and to supposedly protect endangered species.

As documented in the lawsuit filed by the NGO Survival International in the International Court of Human Rights in The

Hague, the double WWF, these philanthropists of the green mafia hired mercenaries to sexually abuse, torture and mass murder the indigenous hunting tribes of the jungle, a genocide in the name of defending pseudo-animal rights, but hey, we'll have to develop this later, so let's return to the course of Bill Gates' particular adventure in Africa for 2010. Bill appointed the head of It pleases Dr. Robert Jorge, a former Monsanto executive who was the author of Ramdac , the most widely used herbicide on the planet, which contains a substance called Poe 15, capable of generating diarrhea, dizziness, shortness of breath, colic and long-term cancer cells. . By the way, the tests on the toxicity of Ramdac are much higher than those that exist against the common glyphosate where there are more rumors than evidence. By then, 70% of AGRA's white elephant grantees in Kenya were working directly with Monsanto seed, and nearly 80% of Gates Foundation funding was in biotechnology and bio-experimentation.

You can be a guinea pig either to feed us or to heal us, in this regard we recommend you read the book "The Constant Gardener", the providential novel by the British ex-spy John Le Carré, where he narrates the inhuman experimentation with humans, involuntary, hidden and totally malicious and planned by various English laboratories, implemented on the soil of their former African colonies during the 1990s. Bill Gates may have read the book as an instruction manual. By the way, promoting Monsanto was not a free choice, since precisely in that year Gates multiplied his shareholding in the company, adding 50,000 shares of this monopoly intrinsically linked to the state underworld, since Monopolies are not caused by the market but always built from the state.

True to his style, Bill not only did not respond to the numerous claims about these irregularities in Africa, but he himself filmed commercial advertising spots selling Monsanto as the final solution to the problem of hunger, something that reminds Jonathan Swift, who stated in his ironic essay, that he had the final solution to child hunger in Ireland, which was to kill half the poor children and feed the other half with their bodies. Of course, in Swift's case it was satire and in Gates's case, everything that seems like a joke is a real tragic nightmare today. Thanks to Gates' intervention, Monsanto, which already has its representation on the board, produces half the calories consumed in the world's poorest countries.

It should be remembered that the rise of this corporation occurred in the context of another war, that of Vietnam, when its main product was Agent Orange, a herbicide with high concentrations of dioxins that allowed the degradation of the Vietnamese forests where the Vietcong guerrillas were hiding. . Who bought it? Obviously a single client, the same client that we previously told you that bought Bill Gates' technological helmets, that is, the United States Army. The irony is that those who would prosecute Monsanto would not be the Vietnamese children burned alive by the herbicide, nor the elderly Vietnamese who perished by starvation, but the US veterans themselves, who experienced more than 20 diseases caused by Agent Orange such as cleft lip, cleft palate, clefts in the spine, immune deficiencies, nervous disorders, diabetes and Parkinson 's .

Attentive Spaniards, Gates and Monsanto began their first joint experiment before Agra, specifically in your nation in Spain with BT 176 corn, which contains genes from jellyfish, insects and bacteria. The European Union banned it in 2005 and this forced the disposal of more than 60,000 hectares in the Iberian Peninsula.

Thanks to their production, the owners of the farms waged a hundred lawsuits for fraud against these failed seed sellers, who are much more terrorists than businessmen. What seduced Gates from Monsanto was its peculiar patent system, much more aggressive even than Microsoft's. The problem has never been the transgenic technologies that are part of the miracle that allows feeding 8,000 million mouths, when a century ago there were barely 1,000 million. The problem is monopolies, the annihilation of competition that allows these gentlemen to sell products of the worst quality at the highest price, since buyers have no one else to turn to.

Monsanto, Gates, the Rockefellers, the Rothschilds and other people belonging to the financial and technological elites use technology that was developed from free knowledge of all kinds, physics, biology, chemistry, engineering, etc., knowledge for which no one charged them , ideas like those of Darwin and Wallace, which appear and are formulated by different people simultaneously, even if they do not know each other, but the state allows them to appropriate these ideas to their friends, of course, in an illegitimate way and through violence of the law, forcing millions of producers around the world to not be able to do what Gates and Monsanto are allowed, turning peasants into forced clients, into slaves.

Patents are not an invention of industrial capitalism that flourished in Germany, England or decentralized Italy hand in hand with permanent competition and permanent changes in the bourgeois class system. Patents are an occurrence of the Jacobin intellectuals of the French Revolution, undisputed fathers of modern socialism and affected by all kinds of centralized control of societies, political centralization, economic centralization, food centralization. Before Monsanto, the rest of the biotech companies were governed by the doctrine of exhaustion, which meant that their patents expired when the product was sold to the end user. Monsanto revolutionized this patent concept by hiring an army of lawyers, lobbyists, prosecutors and judges in 112 countries, where it managed to impose a pseudo patent law that even covers third or fourth generation seeds.

Organizations like the European Patent Office tried to ban Monsanto from patenting plants, animals. However, Monsanto found a way to circumvent this measure through legal loopholes, so that if patenting conventionally produced plants is prohibited, we will patent plants and animals created entirely by genetic engineering, as you hear it, here is when the terrifying and apparently delirious projects that later appeared on the part of Bill Gates, such as artificial dairy products or test-tube meat.

Don't think that Gates just took over the transport infrastructure in Africa. In April 2011, the Microsoft co-founder became the largest shareholder in Canadian National Railway , Canada's largest railway company, for a value of 3.2 billion Canadian dollars that allowed it to acquire enough shareholding power to decide its fate. The presence of the Canadian National Railway is not limited to Canada, since today the Canadian National Railway is known as the great North American railroad, standing out in the United States, where it maintains a line that connects Montreal with New Orleans, carrying all kinds of products and also passengers. Today it is the only company that crosses the country from the Atlantic to the Pacific coast, linking Halifax and Vancouver, and again it is a regulated business that is only possible in this degree of concentration thanks to the political authority of the transportation.

In the beginning, the railways were born with absolute freedom of enterprise, allowing the exponential economic development of North American capitalism long before the Government put their hands there, and it was precisely the Rockefellers of the 19th century, among others, who once convinced that the The best business was to exterminate their competitors, they manipulated the politicians and demanded the creation of a regulatory trust that ended up extremely concentrating the sector. Only they could pay for the regulations and that is how they annihilated the others, giving way then, because they wanted to, to an artificially increased demand for cars and trucks, where they were already doing their new business.

Curiously, Warren Buffett, Gates's friend, until the most recent scandals that persuaded him to keep his distance, became the owner of the only real competitor of the Canadian, we refer to the Burlington Northern Santa Fe, and playing with them as if

North America were a Monopoly board , in 2012 the two friends Gates and Buffett already concentrated more than half of the total length of the railway network 84 of the existing 153,000 km.

In 2013 at the gates of the Russian annexation of Crimea, again what a magnificent coincidence, Bill Gates had an idea thinking that if he already had the seeds and he already had the transport, what he now needed was land to cultivate. So Bill took the next step and began buying land starting in 2013 through Derek Jurosek , the chief operating officer of his personal fund, Cascade Investment , Jurosek himself confirms . But Gates asked him for maximum discretion to keep it a secret until well into 2014, the year in which Henry Kissinger, hired as an advisor to Cascade Investment and at the same time a close consultant to Putin, had predicted to Gates that the Euromaidan crises would break out in Ukraine . and the subsequent conflict between Russia and Ukraine; crises that have been a success, since there is nothing like a business run by its own owners, which also works for planned wars.

The situation gained public relevance when the Quarterman firm received a tip that Cascade Investments was buying his first fields in Ohio, when the people of Quarterman began to search the local property registries, they found that all roads ended with whom they least imagined: Bill Gates, until then known at least in the United States as the archetypal tech tycoon. It turns out that in all the states where the Gates couple had acquired fields, there was a complex network of shell companies to get around the restrictive ceilings against large estates. In other words, the limits to amassing large tracts of land by Uncle Sam of the Washington DC Federal Government. While these companies did not explicitly name Cascade investment , they shared the same mailing address in Kirkland , Washington state, with the address of none other than the headquarters of the Bill & Melinda Gates Foundation, often registering neither more nor less that the e-mail addresses taken from the website belong to the domain of this foundation, so the truth is that they did not make too much effort to hide it, beyond the fact that this served to make some dim-witted official of the North American government dizzy.

All the large acreage linked to the Gates was in turn enrolled in a high-tech sustainability program that included specific drones to monitor cultivation. Chips for cattle and mutant seeds. If you are reading this from the United States, you should know that it is very likely that you have been consuming one of Bill Gates' vegetables for years. The Stanley Farms farm specializes in onions, the Cojin farm Farms in carrots, and others are in charge of corn, wheat, soybeans and potatoes. Each and every one of the items that are becoming stratospherically more expensive from the current Putin invasion. In this way, Joe Biden calls on Congress to substitute imports in the best Peronist style, which would further increase the prodigious profits in his base state, which is Washington. Gates owns over 14,000 acres devoted to GM potatoes, which are so large they're even visible from satellites in outer space. The ironic thing is that many of them end up being processed as French fries for a very healthy company that everyone knows, which is none other than McDonald's . Gates asks that we eat less meat, but he sells his parents to the largest corporate buyer of beef on the planet.

It shouldn't surprise us that the test-tube McBills will soon be inaugurated and what better than a McBill accompanied by a Gates coke. It's no joke, the landowner also owns 1.3% of the shares of Coca-Cola Femsa , the exclusive distributor of the brand's soft drinks, bottled waters and juices in Mexico, Guatemala, Nicaragua, Nicaragua, Costa Rica, Panama, Colombia, Maduro's Venezuela, Brazil and Argentina. Coca Cola Femsa is the largest bottler in the world, that is, it uses plastic and oil, and its parent company, Coca Cola Company, is considered the largest plastic polluter due to the 100,000 single-use disposable plastic bottles it sells each year, which is another chapter of the selective environmentalism of Mr. Gates. None of this keeps him up at night, though, as Gates quenches your thirst with his sodas, grows your vegetables, and they get to you through their own logistical means.

On the other hand, the Walmart chain is the fifth largest share of the Gates Foundation stock portfolio with more than 11,600,000 titles. Walmart is a giant with supermarkets in 27 countries, which guarantees it the first place in the ranking of the sector in Fortune magazine , while Walmart for a change also leads another ranking, the ranking of environmental pollution. According to the metrics of the Pacific Environment , Walmart leads the world's top companies that emit greenhouse gases, including jin , sulfur oxide and nitrous oxide and surpassing Jeff Bezos's Amazon by 7 boxes, another great green activist with whom Gates shares the ultra-elitist aviation project, ZeroAvia , which is about making 10 times more expensive hydrogen-powered planes that could only carry 50 passengers instead of the 500 or 600 traditionally carried by conventional lines. On what does the existence and growth of ZeroAvia depend ? Of course, on the bureaucratic obstacles to conventional air navigation, that is, to the regular airlines that most people use.

We can already see a resigned Boris Johnson in England, where many are wondering why they signed Brexit, if now the owner of their sovereignty is Bill Gates, and we can also see Emmanuel Macron, who was narrowly re-elected in France. We can also see Pedro Sánchez who, unfortunately for the Spanish, continues to lead the social communist coalition that squeezes its citizens with taxes among other ways. These three presidents implement laws that severely restrict flights of less than two hours in their nations, of those planes used by the majority of people not as wealthy as these political or technocratic elites who use exclusive "ecological" private jets.

This measure, which aims at a total ban on conventional flights by 2040, helps neither more nor less than to enrich Gates in the kingdom of heaven, at least on earth. In the same way, they do the same by restricting in these countries the normal classic fossil fuel cars in favor of electric cars, a business where

Gates, especially since he became involved in the Covid vaccines , is the most favored rich man along with Elon Musk. Why? Because the Break Through Energy Coalition that Gates leads is the number 1 strategist in the world lithium market, an ultra-polluting component, by the way, with which not only telephone and computer batteries are made, but also those for electric cars. Everything agrees.

For that reason we are going to talk a little about Break Through Energy Ventures, which is the largest coalition of millionaires ever created. Their stated goal is to support green innovation and all sustainable energy technology, but behind the marketing we see a club that includes Facebook's Mark Zuckerberg, who also owns Instagram and WhatsApp, Alibaba's Jack Ma , George Soros and of course , to Bill Gates, who has been chosen by the rectorate of this select as executive president. These VIP bandits manage 80 companies in 11 countries spread over four continents and chose for the launch of this monumental feat the announcement of their greatest achievement, the United Nations 2030 agenda. Agenda 2015 and Agenda 2030 plus Break Through Energy Ventures are two brands to call the same product: unsustainable underdevelopment for the benefit of very few. George Lucas, the director of the Star saga, recently joined Break Through Energy Ventures. Wars . But another much more central piece of information, nothing anecdotal, is the presence of a Ukrainian partner in both Break Through Energy Ventures and The giving Pledge , the oldest club of philanthropists founded by Bill Gates together with his friend Warren Buffett, has a peculiar associate who is Victor Pinchuk , who is a Ukrainian oligarch who has an estimated fortune of 1,440 million dollars and whose investment holding company owns four channels where in all, without exception, products from the company of Zelenski , the current president of Ukraine, have been bought, when this company in 1995 had headquarters in Moscow and contracts directly with Putin. Pinchuk also controls the main steel and wheel production company in Ukraine and the main public concessionaire for hydraulic infrastructure and engineering services.

By the way Pinchuk was a member of the Ukrainian parliament from 1998 to 2006. All these oligarchs are politicians like Putin's best friend Zelensky has in jail. Pinchuk is married to Elena Kuchma, the daughter of former Ukrainian President Leonid Kuchma, a Putin stooge who ended up implicated in the murder of journalist Georgiy Gongadze , whose body was found in a Kiev forest just two weeks after he had secretly recorded conversations exposing Kuchma's corruption.

Pinchuk couple can be seen in a photo posing with Bill plus former British minister Tony Blair, Richard Branson and Muhammad Yunus. Pinchuk and his wife have their own philanthropic foundation, the Pinchuk Foundation , which has even donated $25 million to the Clinton Foundation and about $150,000 to Donald Trump so he doesn't feel offended. As if that were n't enough Pinchuk integrates as director the round table of the Davos Forum or World Economic Forum, which he personally attended to give a speech on Ukraine in 2013. While in 2016 when he had already signed up for the humanitarian campaign of Gates and Buffet pinchuk was accused of corruption in the special control commission of the ukrainian parliament for receiving a bribe of 5 million dollars a month, in exchange for delivering under the table the right to manage 51% of Booker Nafta, the company Ukraine's largest state-owned company, which is responsible for carrying out about 91% of the country's oil extraction and 27% of the country's natural gas. According to the Prosecutor's Office, an equivalent of 110 million dollars was transferred by Pinchuk to offshore companies, inflicting a serious wound, a mortal wound on the Ukrainian energy sector, whose last owners were the Pinchuk oligarch himself and his father-in-law, the murderer of journalists, Leonid Kuchma. Pinchuk has been branded a traitor to Ukraine after publishing an article in the Wall Street Journal in 2016 claiming that Ukraine had to make painful compromises to achieve peace with Russia. In other words, surrender to the demands of Vladimir Putin and never join the European Union, never join NATO and hand over Donbass and Crimea on a silver platter. The then president of Ukraine, Petro Poroshenko , raised a claim with the World Economic Forum that his most prominent Ukrainian exponent, Pinchuk himself, was openly operating against the interests of his country. His request was completely ignored and Poroshenko , as an act of protest, decided not to participate in the Davos meeting in 2017 to avoid crossing paths with the traitor Pinchuk and also as a gesture of contempt for Klaus Schwab. And you may be wondering what role Pinchuk is playing today?.

Pinchuk , the Ukrainian partner of Putin and Bill Gates, has given a twofold answer regarding the Russo-Ukrainian war. First, the Pinchuk Foundation has made it a priority to help the Zelensky government through a contemporary art show sponsored by Elton John, a friend of Bill Gates and Pinchuk . That's how they laundered money, sorry, they raised funds to assist the victims of the Russian-Ukrainian war through the sale of paintings and contemporary structures. The curious leader of the resistance, Zelenski , took time to thank Pinchuk for this gesture, since Zelenski 's own millionaire personal fortune derives from bribes for renewed state contracts to characters like Igor Kolomoiski or Pinchuk himself , and to the rest of the mafia ruling class of the Eastern European country, Ukraine.

Therefore, far from expelling the Putin collaborator, Pinchuk was rewarded with a key agreement: that of hydropower. Do you remember that in a suicidal, absurd and inexplicable way, Zelensky decided to drown the black Ukrainian plains, the sources of the bulk of the Ukrainian national wealth? Actually there is an explanation for this fact and it is called Bill Gates, translated into Ukrainian Víktor Pinchuk , the beneficiary of the 44 million euros used to divert the Niter River, loosely emulating the tactic applied by the Dutch to stop the savage aggression of the Spanish Tercios in the 16th century. But the Netherlands of that time had much less to lose than the Ukrainians of today, who with this tactic of flooding are giving up their source of livelihood, which is food production.

Across the border, another personal friend of Gates, Vladimir Potanin , a member of The giving Pledge rubs his hands over the biggest tragedy of 2022 which is the Ukraine war. Potanin is a graduate of the Diplomatic Academy of the Soviet State Institute, and he worked for the Schwab lobby in the 1990s. And before that he went through the Ministry of Foreign Affairs of the Soviet Union, and most likely had contact with that executive committee. of Jeffrey Epstein, Bronfman and Soros from the 80s of the 20th century. Also Potanin worked for Klaus Schwab's lobby as soon as the Berlin Wall fell, and became Boris Yeltsin's deputy prime minister, months before handing over to his close friend, Anatoli Chubais. Potanin left office in 1997 to work actively in the Soros group because his stay in this holding company is not an assumption, but a proven fact that even appears in the biography of Potanin on Wikipedia in English. The following year, Potanin and Soros took care of articulating the financial debacle of the Russian banking system, the famous Russian crisis of 1998. Naturally, Putin has not deported Potanin either, nor has he imprisoned him or poisoned him, on the contrary he recruited him to work in their ranks. Today Potanin is literally the richest man in Russia or at least on paper, given that 80% of his fortune, he told the Ria Novosti agency , stems from his strategic deals with the Kremlin.

Potanin plays hockey with Putin three times a year, vacations together on the Black Sea, and in fact employs one of his two daughters at a millionaire salary for a totally unknown role.

In other words, Putin and Potanin do not hide their close relationship and despite this almost carnal brotherhood with President Putin, he is benefiting more than anyone else from the war. The European business press is beginning to wonder why the richest man in Russia does not lose his fortune, but on the contrary, it multiplies it from the sanctions. One of the explanations is that Potanin is buying foreign banks that are leaving, such as the French General Company, at a bargain price, and his influence in the Eurasian country continues to grow.

As a good friend of Chubáis , Potanin also has his leg in the other hemisphere since he is a member of the Council on Foreign Relations run by Kissinger, is a member of the Bilderberg Club and donates to the Kennedy Center for Visual Arts. Also to the surprise of some, Potanin finances the anti-corruption data collective, of course, so that the collective does not collectivize its own corruption data. While lately, Vladimir Potanin is expanding his portfolio at Rosbank, TSC Group Holding and other banks, which are the ones that process payments for key imports from Russia. It is no coincidence that the second most significant US product behind automobiles in imports requiring government authorization is immune products and food biotechnology. Guess who is the main supplier of this combined item that moves an average of 270 million dollars annually?. Of course it's Gates. So the Ukrainian putinist (Putin friend and supporter) Pinchuk , Potanin and Bill Gates have long been in charge of creating another type of bank, the so-called world seed vault.

With the support of Monsanto and Rockefeller, these three magnates inaugurated the Svalbard project in Norway, which is a kind of Noah's ark, located 800 miles from the North Pole, in which 250 million variants of seeds, in order to preserve the genetic material in the face of a possible climatic or nuclear apocalypse like the one that the Russian government is threatening day after day in recent weeks. In fact, if a world atomic war broke out, and the United States and Russia used only half of their arsenal, 750 million people would die as a result of the bombs themselves. Radiation and the rest of its immediate effects would produce four times more deaths, that is, more than 3,000 million.

Of the 8,000 million that inhabit this world, many would eventually die of hunger, since possibly the worst consequence of a nuclear escalation would be precisely the rendering useless of the lands of the broad continental regions that would be affected, and this is in accordance with the consensus of experts from both sides. Thus, there is no room for discussion. The worst effect of a nuclear winter would be brought about by the food issue.

As if that were not enough, Gates decided that Break Through Energy should also advance on water. He himself introduced Janicki Omniprocessor , a machine that transforms waste into supposedly drinkable water and electricity. With his classic charisma to which we are accustomed, Bill appeared in a video drinking a glass of water, which 5 minutes ago was human feces. To double the bet, years later, he presented another project that basically consisted of a toilet that worked without water, a toilet that was not connected to any sewage system and that was capable of transforming human waste into alternative fertilizers, which seemed like a delusion for that So, however, today it begins to look like a brilliant business idea. Repentant observers at the Luxenburg Foundation published a report titled False Promises for 2020, before the mass lockdown in which Gates played a role no one is unaware of anymore. The 14th anniversary of the Agra project in Africa was completed and the number of Africans suffering from extreme famine, far from having decreased, had increased by 30% in the 18 countries that Gates targeted, such as Mali, Tanzania, Zambia and Kenya . Rural poverty spread dramatically and the number of destitute hungry people in these nations rose to 131 million human beings, which is an illustration of what the 2030 agenda brings.

The Luxembourg Foundation study also reveals a diversion of funds theoretically intended for Africans, but which ended, or rather, never left the United States and Europe. Funding focused much more on state policy making than on agriculture itself.

Australian MP Dan Andrews, a member of the World Economic Forum, recently introduced a bill praised by Gates, which includes a ban on home gardens. Australia is the country that could, but did not want to stop the extradition of one of the greatest heroes in its history, Julian Assange. The same government of Scott Morrison, which prohibited a large part of its citizens, those who were not willing to trust Bill Gates and his compulsory state policies, from even going to buy food in stores, are also the same politicians of the Australian anti-liberal party that treated the tennis player Novak Djokovic as a war criminal, who was deported.

Another example of how farmers' dollars ended up anywhere but in farmers' pockets was the forum titled High-Level Dialogue on Food in Africa, a conglomerate of 18 African heads of state and most notable of all was that each of the exhibitors received millionaire funds from Gates. However, none of its nations improved the poverty figures one iota.

This twisted "success" of Agra in Africa gave a new impetus to the Gates Foundation, which announced its next international but Americas-focused evolution, Gates AG One , as the Covid pandemic flooded and possessed televisions around the world. world in January 2020, Gates was hatching his next plan. Continuing the tradition, he put Joe Cornelius, Monsanto's former director of international development, at the helm of Gates AG One . Like Agra, Gates AG One maintains that it seeks to empower small farmers, but this time with state-of-the-art technologies linked to the so-called Internet of Things, framed in the fourth anti-industrial revolution of the Great Reset , promoted by its usual sponsors of the Davos Forum, and validated one by one all these tools as instruments to implement the objectives of its unsustainable development of the 2030 agenda.

In addition to everything they did in Africa, they now add the introduction of a totalitarian surveillance system where ranchers and farmers will not be able to grow seeds or graze herds unless their system approves, the so-called agriculture 3.0. In this way, the activist Vandana Shiva affirms that the real reason for this advance is to know thoroughly the practices, the traditions, the secrets, the best knowledge of each farmer to select those that are useful for Gates' social engineering, and to prohibit or restrict through economic or legislative blackmail, those that are disposable or hindering.

This experience of collected data will continue to accumulate progressively and will return to the farmers in the form of strict programs, which in turn will govern their new ways of producing, something reminiscent of Stalin's five-year plans, the result of which was what historians baptized as the Great Famine.

Complementary to Gates AG One is AgTech Accelerator, a research grant focused on developing machines that automate all stages of food production. This aims to eradicate rural human labor and, therefore, the life of the country man, in other words, to empty the countryside of the last redoubt of freedom in the face of the metastasis of socialist cancer, with the ultimate goal of connecting the seeds directly to internet and be able to harvest through an app managed by a smartphone. Gates made a strong incursion into Latin America, accelerating the modernization of agriculture.

In this way, in 2020, the Government of Alberto Fernández, president of Argentina, who boasted that older adults are a cost and a serious problem, while now Gates and his friends maintain that the elderly are a climate problem. The same Government of Alberto Fernández that without blushing handed over to George Soros the state indoctrination apparatus calling itself the Ministry of Education, Alberto Fernández himself. That same model progressive government admired by López Obrador, Gustavo Petro, Gabriel Boric or Pedro Castillo, signed with Gates the implementation of a program called AgTech , which had the support of the local pharmaceutical tycoon Hugo Sigman , heir to the historical treasurer of the Argentine Communist Party. , who was his father-in-law, Silvio Golf.

In other words, Gates AG One is already in Argentina hand in hand with the OAS and the State. While in Mexico, López Obrador, who has signed the juiciest contracts in the history of Microsoft in the subcontinent, has done his thing with AgTech Mex, which has a network made up of 200 Morena entrepreneurs. He did it in the same way that he handed over the management of the Covidd plandemic to the Gates Foundation . The fourth transformation is the upward transformation of the profits of the tycoon Bolsonaro , another demagogue who says a lot but always does the exact opposite, being the first of all these officials to accept the experimental package. Brazil already in 2019 had a record of 125 ArTech firms that worked together with Cargill, the largest marketer of soybeans and accused, by the way, of much of the deforestation of the Amazon.

In February 2021, Gates was found with a net worth of $121 million, but for the first time with an incredibly significant component of rural properties spread across 19 US states, and occupying an area similar to 7 times Manhattan, more than 242,000 acres that establish him as the largest landowner in the United States. The great unknown is, if it was so difficult to discover his land purchase network in his native country, how many more will Gates own in the rest of the world without us knowing yet?

By May 2021, the Gates rail network was annexed by Kansas City Southern , the major railroad company in the South. It was the largest rail agreement of the 21st century and plans to build the first network to connect Canada, the United States and Mexico. In less than 12 months Bill Gates managed to make his shares rise 31%.

Biden succeeded more than Gates, since the Democratic president had already presented a striking investment of 80,000 million to ecologically renovate and enlarge the federal train network passing through Nashville, Atlanta, Houston and Dallas. How could it be otherwise, Biden 's very expensive reform was financed by the Americans.

By the way, Gates is not a vegan, nor is he a vegetarian, although he tried during his youth, lasting only a year without eating hamburgers. This personal hobby was not an impediment for him to now try to prohibit the rest of us from consuming beef, repeating the usual formula ad infinitum, either with Windows or with whatever, the reality is that Gates wants us to eat his meat, if you can call what is produced by the Californian company Beyond Meat , which sells a meat substitute item. Its creators spent five years perfecting non-meat proteins with the patronage of Gates, who said that he ventured to try a taco of this pseudo chicken from this pseudo company, and that he could not tell if it was real or fake, which we do not know. We believe it very much, but it can be something fascinating for vegan influencers and the same animalists who rape and murder children in Africa.

By the way , this product is already sold in several Walmart branches, and even in countries like Singapore or the United Arab Emirates it is easier to find in vitro meat, test-tube meat, fake meat, than real meat. But unfortunately for Bill, this meat substitute did not have the best reception from food critics, and in this way a culinary review of the newspaper Lemont comments that "the best thing I can say about Beyond Meat , is that your product looks like the worst chicken I've ever tasted." While Manuel Collado, a Spanish scientist specialized in cancer, pointed out that in vitro meat can be a lethal weapon. He said that it must be taken into account that it is about ingesting the bovine tissue that starts from living pluri potential cells with tumor capacity, and maintained with growth factors and agents of untested capacity. Similar opinions have been issued so far by the rest of the specialized scientific community, for example, the lapidary sentence of the Nuffield Council on Bioethics , which said the potential for contamination and bacterial growth in the cultivation process carries a high risk to consumer health.

During the last interview that the stellar protagonist Gates granted to his colleagues at the World Economic Forum, he indicated that all countries should consume 100% synthetic meat, words that were echoed by the Spanish Minister of Consumer Affairs, the communist Alberto Garzón , which consumes what it claims to repudiate: the iPhone, alcohol and ham.

In the same Davos Forum interview, Gates proposed introducing legislation that would restrict the demand for meat and thus shift it towards the consumption of pseudo-meat. They don't want to let us even enjoy roast meat, bread, water and wine.

As a final reflection, we tell you that during the time it has taken you to read this book, more than 500 cows have died due to the grain shortage caused by the war, which is Bill Gates' war, and it is not against Ukraine, but against all humanity.

FINAL CONCLUSION

As the Russian-Ukrainian war has been proven to be planned and fabricated in advanced in this book, so it happens with most wars, food, energy and financial crises, etc.

Similarly, each phase of the 2030 globalist agenda is "predicted" by a simulated pandemic, famine, etc. be it the 201 Event for the Coronavirus pandemic, the Food Chain Reaction for the food crisis, or the monkeypox pandemic, for which a document was also published in March 2021, with the agenda for the expansion of this pandemic from May 15, 2022, just when it broke out, until December of 2023.

There is a lot of evidence to certify that there is a strategy underway to terrorize the population, prepare it to accept a WHO global health government, submit to a new mass vaccination campaign, and help pharmaceutical companies to continue making money, while the terrible side effects of their products are hidden.

Sometimes the globalist agenda may meet with some resistance from the national agendas of other countries such as Russia or China, but always the elites and politicians take advantage of each other's agendas.

In this case, the current crisis is about the survival of the dollar as a world reserve currency, about NATO's control of the world over China and Russia, the latter being the declared enemy of NATO since its very foundation, about the fight for the world finances of the Western bloc led by the United States and Europe against the Eastern bloc led by China and Russia, etc.

The 2030 globalist agenda continues with its version 2.0. or the second part, changing the scenarios and introducing other plandemics (planned pandemics) after Covid , climate change and any excuse to achieve their goals: control and impoverish the majority of citizens by establishing a supranational world government not elected by the people, because the increase in energy and food prices affects the poor and middle classes but little to the richest classes, politicians and large corporations, which also have special privileges in terms of paying taxes, or life pensions.

In short, the hunger games of the 2030 agenda have begun, and what seemed like science fiction movies has become a reality.

If the elites that organize these simulations of pandemics, famines and misfortunes were really looking out for the good of humanity, with these simulations they would be able to avoid the misfortunes that they simulate for the near future, but nevertheless all their predictions of misfortunes are produced equally, for then the ruling classes and the elites go on to act after the crises that they theoretically predict, but which they obviously organize themselves, break out. Therefore, obviously the globalist elites of the World Economic Forum, the Bilderberg Club, the Bill and Melinda Gates Foundations, the Rockefeller Foundation, the Soros Open Society , and many other globalist organizations, etc. They do not have the good-natured intentions they claim to have, but the opposite.

BIBLIOGRAPHY AND SOURCES CONSULTED

- Rand Corporation report " Overextending and unbalancing Russia". Original English title " Overextending and unbalancing Russia ", dated January 1, 2019.

- Report "NATO 2030: United for a new era." Analysis and recommendations of the reflection group appointed by the Secretary General of NATO", dated November 25, 2020. The original title in English is: NATO 2030: United for a new era. Analysis and recommendations of the reflection group appointed by the NATO secretary general.

- César Vidal TV's Great Reset Programs : NATO's Financial War Against Russia Drives the Great Globalist Reset, NATO 2030: World War III for a New Globalist Era, The Great Famine: Crisis Manufactured to Expand the Globalist Agenda, The Real hunger games: globalist simulacrum designed in 2015.

- Documentary film: "Search, find, tell" by Alexander Alexanyan.

- Videos from the YouTube channel "Los Liberales" by Nicolás Morás : "The secret alliance of Putin and Bill Gates" and "The final blow of the elite. Bill Gates is going for your food."

ABOUT THE AUTHOR

César Madrigal

César Madrigal has a degree in Management and Public Administration from the University of Barcelona, speaks English, French, Italian and German, and is passionate about studying and researching on international economics and politics. In 2017 he published his first book on Amazon titled "The dark side of trading and of  financial markets. How I lost all my savings and what I learned from it. ", based on his own experience with short-term speculative investments, proving with the publication of this book a great ability to analyze data, relate it with one another and put it in writing in an understandable and orderly way .

Starting in 2021, he began writing the series of books on the Globalist Agenda, that is, on the New World Order, inspired mainly by the devastating effects on the economy, and the loss of rights of human beings caused by the Covid-19 pandemic, which was planned in advanced by the elites as It is proven in his books, showing great knowledge on the subject.

BOOKS IN THIS SERIES

The globalist agenda is real and dangerous. The great friendship between the Great Reset and the Covid-19.

As the then president of the United States, Barack Obama, wrote on May 16, 2013 on his Twitter account: "Ninety-seven percent of scientists agree that climate change is real, man-made and dangerous", the title of this book series extracts the idea from that famous tweet, because the reality is that there is not a consensus of 97% of scientists that climate change is caused by man and dangerous, even if it has been. announced for decades by the main media constantly and continuously, which has made it over time, without our realizing it, an unquestionable truth accepted by the majority of the population. The theory of global warming or now called climate change, is simply one of the dogmas of a globalist agenda imposed by supranational entities to achieve their goals, and it is really this agenda that is real, man-made and dangerous. People who do not believe in the dangerous global warming theory are often branded as deniers, or as "conspiranoics" (that believe in conspiracy theories) those who believe in the existence of a New World Order imposed on nations, but the truth is that the existence of this agenda and his not very good intentions are increasingly out of the question. In this way the famous billionaire, David Rockefeller, a member of several globalist entities founded in the 20th century, including the Council on Foreign Relations, the Bilderberg Club, and the Trilateral Commission, stated in his memoir published in 2002: "They accuse me of working against the United States and of being an internationalist having created a global economy and politics, not only do I plead guilty for it but I feel proud". Therefore, from this statement we get two basic ideas: the first is that the globalist agenda exists, and second that it goes against the interests of sovereign nations, which of course shows that their intentions are rather evil. While in the second book we are going to see how the globalist agenda begins with the deception of the monetary and financial system that creates money out of thin air and allows States to borrow more and more, public debt that ultimately has to be paid by taxpayers of the middle classes through taxes, which progressively impoverishes them, while the central banks are led by the Group of 30, G30, which is basically made up of central bank bankers and the large international banks, whose executing agency is the bank of central banks, the Bank for International Settlements, BIS. We will also discover that financial elites want to eliminate cash to control us even more through the creation of government-backed Fiat digital currencies, and that cryptocurrencies are therefore a good option to escape this control by the globalist oligarchies. We will also analyze the figure of Bill Gates, the founder of Microsoft, a philanthropist who has actively participated in the definition of that unique thought of the globalist agenda that invades us today, through his projects at the Bill and Melinda Gates Foundation, the Alliance for Global Vaccination (Gavi), the lie and truth about the microchips of Bill Gates's vaccines that are not actually in vaccines but in contraceptive pills, synthetic DNA, his defense of measures to stop the supposed global warming and Microsoft's alliance with news corporations, technological and social media companies, along with the financing of other large technological companies to verify the truth of the news which is rather the censorship of the XXI century, called "fact-checking", from its sender to its receiver.

The Globalist Agenda Is Real And Dangerous. The Great Friendship Between The Great Reset And The

Covid-19.

Just as the then president of the United States, Barack Obama, wrote on May 16th, 2013 on his Twitter account: "Ninety-seven percent of scientists agree that climate change is real, man-made and dangerous ", so the title of this book extracts the idea from that famous tweet, though the reality is that there is no such consensus of 97% of scientists that climate change is man-made and dangerous, though this message has been transmitted for decades by the mainstream media constantly and continuously, which has made it over time, without us realizing of it, an unquestionable truth accepted by the majority of the population.The theory of global warming or now called climate change, is simply one of the dogmas of a globalist agenda imposed by supranational entities to achieve their goals, and it is really this agenda that is real, man-made and dangerous.People who do not believe in the dangerous global warming theory are often branded as deniers, whereas those who believe in the existence of a New World Order imposed on nations as conspiracy believer people, but the truth is that the existence of this agenda and his not very good intentions are increasingly out of the question. Thus, the famous billionaire, David Rockefeller, a member of several globalist entities founded in the 20th century, including the Council on Foreign Relations, the Bilderberg Club and the Trilateral Commission, stated in his "Memoirs" book published in 2002: "Some even believe we (the Rockefeller family) are part of a secret cabal working against the best interests of the United States, characterizing my family and me as 'internationalists' and of conspiring with others around the world to build a more integrated global political and economic structure - one world, if you will. If that's the charge, I stand guilty, and I am proud of it."So from this statement we get two basic ideas: the first is that the globalist agenda exists, and second that it goes against the interests of sovereign nations, which of course indicates that its intentions are not very good.As if it were not enough proof of the existence of the globalist agenda, in 2020 at the World Economic

Forum website it has been published openly and widely on the need for a Great political, economic and social world Reset, obviously imposed without counting on the opinion of ordinary citizens, and the need to take advantage of the Covid-19 pandemic crisis to further promote this great imposed global restart.In addition to man-made global warming, there are other dogmas in the globalist agenda in order to achieve its objectives, such as abortion, euthanasia, massive and uncontrolled migration, the legalization of drug trade, trafficking and consumption, etc. that mainly respond to two objectives of the globalist agenda: the reduction of the world population especially through the promotion of abortion and euthanasia, and the progressive erosion of the values of western democratic nations such as the family, along with the erosion of their national culture and identity, and the emptying of the sovereignty and authority of the national governments that will be transferred to globalist entities, for example through massive and uncontrolled migration or the legalization of drug trafficking and consumption.You might think that these elites who are imposing this agenda have good intentions deep down, since abortion, euthanasia, LGTBIQ + ideology, etc. are presented and defended as human rights of the people. However, these elites are not really interested in defending these rights, but only in what they can achieve with them: subverting the political, social and economic order of the nations in order to justify and achieve a new imposed world order.So the proof that the intentions of these elites are not really the defense of these rights, is that they try to impose an agenda which they have not been voted for.

The Globalist Agenda Is Still Real And Dangerous: The Great Friendship Between The Great Reset And The Covid-19 Continues. Part Ii.

The globalist agenda is still alive and dangerous, and currently its most visible expression is the World Economic Forum, which promotes the Great Reset project in an open and public way, as it can be seen on its own website.

As Mayer Rothschild said more than two centuries ago: "Give me control of a country's money supply and I won't care who makes its laws." In this way this globalist agenda that promotes a new world order in a corporatist socialist system, that is, where the elites rule together with the large technological corporations, begins precisely with the deception of the monetary expansion, in which central banks along with private banks increasingly create more money out of thin air so that the States can borrow more and more, which the middle and lower classes, who are becoming poorer, end up paying with taxes.

In addition, these financial elites led by the Group of Thirty or G30 and whose executing agency is the Bank for International Settlements, also seek greater levels and forms of control with the creation of digital currencies backed by the States with the hidden objective of finishing off with the cash, so today cryptocurrencies such as bitcoin would be a good refuge if this disappearance of the cash happens to occur.

On the other hand, for some time the official media have seen how the population has stopped trusting them when it comes to informing themselves, thus this discrediting of the media together with the need to maintain a single thought on issues such as the activity of the pharmaceutical companies, the effectiveness of the Covid-19 vaccines or the official position regarding the Covid pandemic, for example, has caused the proliferation of an industry of truth-checking companies, called the fact-checking industry, that far from being neutral are often funded by big tech companies to censor dissenting views.

In short, the globalist project these days consists of the concept of inclusive capitalism, in which states and large multinationals join forces to create a new world order, in which fear is used as a weapon to do business and to control the population, which is continually frightened. Thus, Bill Gates already said in a Ted conference in 2015 that the great risk for humanity in the future would not come from any war but from a pandemic; whilst now

Klaus Schwab, the president of the World Economic Forum has said that the next great pandemic much larger than that of Covid-19 will be a cyber pandemic; and in turn the Bank for International Settlements, BIS, says that the next pandemic will be that of the green swan, that is to say that of climate change.